To Liz,
Best wishes,
Jane Duffus

The What The Frock!
Book of Funny Women

By Jane Duffus, Founder of What The Frock! Comedy

GW00670557

Copyright: Jane Duffus

First published in Great Britain in 2015 by BCF Books,
Burton Cottage Farm, East Coker, Somerset BA22 9LS

www.bcfbooks.co.uk

Printed in China through World Print Ltd.

ISBN: 978-0-9571275-0-0

For Paul

and

For Abbie

CONTENTS

FOREWORD BY LUCY PORTER

"I don't usually like female comedians but you were really good."

During the two decades that I've been performing comedy, I have received this 'compliment' dozens of times in comedy clubs. When pressed, the person who says it will usually admit that they've never actually seen another woman perform live comedy. Like gypsies, we female comedians are feared and despised by people who've never actually encountered us in the flesh.

As a fledgling stand-up in the late 1990s, I decided that I would just ignore my gender. When journalists asked the inevitable question, "What's it like being a woman in comedy?" I would curtly reply that I'd never tried being a man in comedy so I had no point of comparison. I used to shun all-female comedy nights because I didn't want to receive special treatment. Anyway, I figured that so many excellent female stand-ups were coming through the ranks that soon people would abandon this ridiculous, outdated notion that women weren't funny.

Of course, with the benefit of hindsight, I realise that I was a massively deluded twit. Thank goodness for people like Jane Duffus who have grasped that if you want to upset the status quo you have to give things at least a nudge in the right direction.

There was much criticism of BBC executive Danny Cohen when he issued a mandate that all TV panel shows should feature at least one woman. I was broadly pleased. Naturally people asked: "Will female comics really want to be seen as the token woman?" I suspect that most of us would rather be seen in any capacity than completely overlooked. Of course, no one wants to feel their success is based on tokenism, or that they are denying opportunities to more talented artists. Luckily comedy is reasonably meritocratic and if you can't make people laugh no amount of positive discrimination will help you.

I was surprised by how much hostility Cohen's edict generated. Some internet commenters went foamy-mouthed at the idea of female preferment. I found their hysteria baffling – we are talking about sticking a few more women on *Mock The Week*, not giving us the nuclear codes. Seems there are still people out there for whom female comics are scary bogeywimmin. They've discovered our secret agenda to outlaw all jokes that aren't about periods and cake, and their cousin once had a lady gagsmith Tarmac his drive really badly.

If you know someone who feels that way about us, why not buy this book for them? It's a great collection of essays on some brilliant comic talents. Obviously, and thankfully, there are hundreds of women who could have been included but weren't. As Jane says, future editions can rectify this, and there are already women I have seen in the comedy clubs this year who might join the pantheon of comedy gods one day.

Lucy Porter
January 2015

INTRODUCTION

*"You are my heroine. And by heroine I mean lady hero.
I don't want to inject you and listen to jazz."*
Liz Lemon, 30 Rock

It is impossible to survive as a woman in the 21st Century without a sense of humour. After all, if you don't laugh… you'll cry.

Comedy endures because it reassures us about who we are and what our place is in this world. A world that is often confusing and complicated, and frequently puts obstacles in the path of our success – but if we can laugh at even the smallest things, we're one step closer to happiness.

When I sat down to write a list of the funniest women I could think of, it became a never-ending task. So I opened it up to the world. At the end of 2012, I created an online survey to find out which women everybody else thought was funny… in the space of a week, more than 500 names were put forward. Some compulsively so (Jennifer Saunders, Dawn French, Victoria Wood, Tina Fey), and some just the once. As well as a few who I'd never previously heard of but have since discovered and enjoyed enormously. It is the results of that survey that spawned the core of this book.

Alongside celebrations of the most popular women comedians to be nominated in the survey, this book also recognises and curtseys before the favourite funny women of 28 fantastic contributors. Those contributors were invited for a number of reasons: because they are comedians themselves (and many have performed with What The Frock!); because they have supported What The Frock! in one way or another in the past few years; and because they do work that I greatly admire and which I feel links to what we're trying to achieve with What The Frock!. I thank them all for their support, both for What The Frock! and for this book.

As well as celebrating the funny women who have gone before us, it's also important to celebrate those still busily working, and a few of the women profiled in this book are relatively early on in what I hope will be long and successful careers. I also wanted to give a few leads to those readers who may be thinking about pursuing stand-up themselves, so at the back of the book are links to suggested further reading that I hope will be helpful.

This book will neither ask nor answer the question 'are women funny?' because of course women are funny. To suggest otherwise is as absurd and as offensive as asking whether a man can be a nurse. This book presumes you know women are funny and simply seeks to confirm this fact and celebrate some of the wonderful women who have made us laugh for the past century or more.

Of course, there's no way one book could possibly include every single funny woman ever. It would result in an enormous book and an impossible task. Instead, this book has cherry picked 71 on the results of that survey, the choices of the contributors and general common sense. There will of course be omissions and maybe your own favourite funny woman isn't in here – that's not because we don't think she's funny or we don't like her, it's simply because there is only so much time and space.

We recognise there is a lack of non-white women in the selection included, and this is not a deliberate omission. We also recognise there is a lack of disabled women, and again this is not deliberate. But we welcome suggestions to remedy this in any future editions.

Jane Duffus, What The Frock! Founder
May 2015

CHAPTER ONE

What is What The Frock! Comedy?

Well, I'm glad you asked. What The Frock! Comedy is a brand that promotes female comedians in an industry that, until very recently, almost compulsively ignores them.

What The Frock! has a monthly club night in Bristol, and has (at the time of writing) expanded to putting on shows in five other UK cities, as well as hosting comedy workshops, solo shows, improv theatre and running an all-female comedy competition that attracts entrants from all around the world. What The Frock! only has one official member of staff (me, Jane), but I am ably supported by an army of many in a variety of capacities. It never ceases to amaze me how wonderful people are with pitching in to help make this happen. And that's what it's all about.

Since January 2012 when I launched What The Frock!, just two people (both men working in the comedy industry) have got in touch to tell me it is sexist to put on events only promoting women. I'd beg to disagree. There are hundreds of men-only comedy nights around the country every single night of the week, but they're just not honest enough to call themselves that. And until this situation changes and comedy clubs book a fair reflection of women comedians there will continue to be women-only comedy events – and What The Frock! is one of three regular events doing this in the UK at the time of writing.

'But are women funny?' 'Do you think it is harder for women than men in the comedy industry?' 'Why don't we see more women comedians?' 'Is women's humour different to men's?' And on and on and on. These are the kind of questions I get asked every week, usually by well meaning people. But these are also the kind of questions that make my heart sink and my jaw clench.

Let me explain…

Back in October 2011, I was at the Cheltenham Literature Festival and I attended an event that involved columnists and broadcasters Grace Dent and Caitlin Moran having a chat for an hour over a bottle of wine. Until that point, it was the funniest and most entertaining hour I'd ever spent as an audience member. Just two women chatting and putting the world to rights, while injecting some dry, witty humour into topics such as the absence of women from TV panel shows and how sub-editors often edited Grace and Caitlin's newspaper columns "to save us from ourselves".

> *"During the Q&A, a woman in the audience suggested Caitlin and Grace should turn this into a TV show as it was so funny and people would love it. A whoop of agreement went up from the sold-out crowd. And of course, the woman who asked this question was right – this would make brilliant TV. However, both Moran and Dent just laughed wryly and said they'd never be allowed to talk in such a candid way on TV… because women never are."*
> MadamJMo blog post, 11 October 2011

On our way home, my husband and I reflected on why this had seemed like such an unusually exciting event. It wasn't hard to work out. It was because it was so rare to see two women being so at ease, so funny and so unselfconsciously intelligent. And the reason we were able to see this was because they hadn't been edited for a TV show or had their words softened by a sub-editor: it was real life. It was so different from what we were normally allowed to see on a stage. If Grace and Caitlin were to do a weekly podcast it would be a huge hit. But all of the successful and popular podcasts we could name (Ricky Gervais, Kevin Smith, Frank Skinner et al) were by men.

On 10 October 2011, I wrote a post on my blog that went viral in hours. It was picked up by *The New Statesman*, *The Guardian*, *The Independent, The Mirror* and more, leading to further articles and debate on those platforms. Within days, it had been read by tens of thousands of people all around the world. And it continues to be the most popular post on my blog and still sees thousands of hits each month.

It was after seeing that event with Grace and Caitlin, via a circuitous route involving Twitter and a lot of moaning, that I set up What The Frock! in January 2012. With the support of Bristol's Festival of Ideas, the first event on 18 May 2012 was intended to be a one-off point-proving exercise. Those points being that there were plenty of funny women out there, and that there was an audience willing to pay to see them. (This was in response to the bookers I had contacted who told me they didn't book many women because there just weren't many women comedians, and that when they did book women they couldn't sell as many tickets as when they booked men comedians). My two points were more than proved. The event at Bristol's Arnolfini sold out 210 seats a week in advance, and the third comedy night had been organised before the first had even happened. It was only meant to be a one-off – but at the time of publication of this book, we're coming up to the fiftieth What The Frock! event! This is for no other reason that an increasing number of people keep buying tickets. We're just, humbly, giving the people what they want to see.

When I'd ask bookers at other comedy clubs and events around the UK why they had so few – if any – women on their bills, the answers were always identical and always defensive. The response to "Why don't you book (m)any women?" always comes in two parts. The first is a huffy: "None of the women we asked were available." Which is baffling, because – as a booker – if I want to book someone for a particular date, and they're not available, I ask someone else who fulfils a similar performance role... rather than give up. The second part to the answer is a snotty: "We do book women actually. And here's a list of the six women we've had on in the past year." What they don't see is that if they also listed the men they'd also had on in the past year of monthly gigs, they wouldn't be listing just six female names... they'd be listing more than 40 male names. But quite simply, the level of annoyance and defensiveness these bookers show me is all I need to see to confirm that they already know they're in the wrong.

In the first year of What The Frock! (2012), we teamed up with not only the Festival of Ideas, but also the international Ladyfest network, UK Feminista and many more organisations. And we hosted charity events in support of the Bristol charity One25, which supports women trapped in street sex work, and the self-explanatorily titled Confronting Women's Poverty event.

In our second year (2013), we began a monthly residency in Bristol (which upscaled to bigger venues twice before the year was through due to continually selling out), and also continued to work alongside the Bristol Festival of Ideas as well as the British Film Institute in London and the Slapstick Festival.... We did our first out-of-Bristol event with a packed performance at the three-day Women of the World Festival at London's Southbank Centre. We were profiled on BBC Radio 4's *Woman's Hour*, as well as featured on BBC TV and in countless national and local press articles, as well as enjoying a regular slot on BBC radio. We also launched the What The Frock! Newcomer Award, cementing our commitment to nurturing up and coming female comedians.

Our third year (2014) saw things move ever onwards as we exceeded 40 events in total. As well as winning our first ever prize (the Venus Award for Customer Service – we were also finalists in the New Business of the Year and Entrepreneur categories), we've continued to work with BBC radio and been the subject of a feature on ITV as well as BBC1. The What The Frock! Newcomer Award returned... this year filling all the places in 10 hours, and receiving applications from as far afield as the States. It turned out that this ladies' comedy thing had legs!

As we go into our fourth year (2015), we're yet again setting up residency in another, even-bigger venue in Bristol, as well as programming events elsewhere in the UK, preparing for the third annual What The Frock! Newcomer Award and, of course, publishing this book. It's an extremely exciting time. And it feels like we've only just started.

The What The Frock! Newcomer Award may not offer fancy prizes or wads of cash, but that's because it is not sponsored. Instead it is one of (at the time of writing) only two all-female comedy competitions in the UK, and as such we offer a friendly and supportive environment to perform and compete, and a judging panel from the BBC. The 2013 award was won by Bethan Roberts, who has gone on to perform with us in three UK cities, been talent spotted by the Bath Comedy Festival and has since played to a sold-out 400-strong audience with us. The 2014 award was won by Dotty Winters, and we have continued to work with Dotty to support her in gaining further exposure and experience.

I recognise that hosting an all-female comedy brand may not be enormously helpful in the long run. By doing so, I'm effectively grouping women together, erecting a big neon arrow and saying, "Oi, look at the funny ladies, they're over here!" But while it remains a fact that on an average Friday night in the UK only 8% of acts performing in clubs will be women... well, I'm going to keep on with what I'm doing [1].

I've asked some of our regular performers and audience members what they'd think about What The Frock! starting to book male acts now and again, and the response is always a firm and solid "no!". So that's me told.

Only a handful of women who I've tried to book for gigs have declined explaining politely that they don't do all-female line-ups, and I respect their decision and understand why. Then again, the majority of women who perform at What The Frock! say they love the atmosphere at all female line-ups and comment on how much more relaxing and supportive it is than at a mixed line-up.

We shouldn't have to segregate the genders in the 21st Century, though. We don't need to return to the Victorian era where boys go to school through one gate and girls through another and never the twain shall meet. But to me the important point is to provide a platform to encourage and nurture new female talent, and to continue to raise the profile of those talented performers in the media. This is what What The Frock! aims to do, and this book is an extension of that goal.

CHAPTER TWO

Where are the women?

"It is a very serious thing to be a funny woman."
Frances Whitcher (American humourist, 1814-1852)

In 2013, Bridget Christie won the Foster's Edinburgh Comedy Award, the biggest prize at the world's biggest comedy festival. She was the third female winner in the (at that time) 33-year history of the award, previously known as the Perrier Prize. Bridget's gender shouldn't need to be remarked upon. What should have led the news stories was that a fantastic comedian had deservedly won a highly contested award at an enormous festival. But instead, that became the secondary story after the fact that Bridget was, gasp, a woman. After Bridget won the Foster's Award, there also can't have been many people left who did not learn that her husband is comedian Stewart Lee. As if the identity of her husband is relevant to her award win.

In the 21st Century, why should a person's gender still precede them? If one of the many male comedians who had performed at Edinburgh in 2013 had won the award, the news stories would not have been "male comedian X was the 30th man to win in the award's 33 year history". You don't hear Peter Kay or Michael McIntyre being introduced as 'male comedians', they're just 'comedians'. Yet the likes of Miranda Hart or Jo Brand will always have to endure their gender being publicised before their job title is.

Until a few years ago, I never realised that almost all of the comedians on the circuit were men. Growing up in the 1980s, the comedians on the telly were people like Ben Elton, Canon and Ball and *The Young Ones*. When the *NME* started banging on in the early 1990s about comedy being the new rock'n'roll, it was acts such as Vic Reeves, Bob Mortimer, Emo Phillips, Robert Newman, David Baddiel and Frank Skinner they were raving about. And when I started going to comedy gigs at university in the late 1990s, I went to see Harry Hill, Robert Newman, Alistair McGowan and co. When I began reviewing comedy professionally from the mid-2000s, I was reviewing Dara O'Briain, Rhod Gilbert, Reginald D Hunter, Jason Byrne… in fact, the only woman I had ever reviewed was Sarah Millican. But I never realised at the time that almost all of those acts were men. It just didn't occur to me. My consciousness had not yet been raised.

What made me realise was joining Twitter in 2010. Twitter is a wonderful space for women to speak, to be funny and to be themselves. Twitter allows women to remain unedited and unconstrained. There is no sub-editor who re-writes a woman's words on Twitter "for her own good" or to "save her from herself", as Grace Dent and Caitlin Moran said in Cheltenham. On Twitter, a woman is free to say what she wants. And as a result, Twitter is populated by gazillions of extremely witty, funny and intelligent women.

The downsides of this free speech for women on Twitter, of course, are the highly publicised death and rape threats that outspoken or influential women are subjected to by the vocal minority who disagree with them. And while it is of course extremely unpleasant for the women receiving such threats and abuse, this does show up how threatened some people still are by intelligent and strong women.

Via Twitter, I grew to love Grace Dent even more (I'd already been loving her columns in *The Guardian* for years), as well as Caitlin Moran and many hundreds more. Via Twitter I met a whole community of virtual friends who were interested in flying the flag for women in the arts and giving women a voice… and through these Twitter friends I joined in the expressions of horror at how few women were appearing on TV and radio shows. Just as I had never previously noticed that I was mostly watching male comedians in theatres, I had also never previously noticed that I was mostly watching and listening to men on shows such as *Have I Got News For You?*, *Mock The Week*, *8 Out Of 10 Cats*, *QI*, *Just A Minute*, *I'm Sorry I Haven't A Clue*… even *Question Time*, *Newsnight* etc rarely had women on. Where were all the women? They couldn't all be tucked away in the kitchen making sandwiches, surely?

Like anything, once your consciousness on a topic has been raised, there's nothing you can do to lower it again. However hard you may want to. I started to see inequality everywhere. And it really wound me up. There was no good reason why women weren't being included. Or that the women who were included on panel shows were mostly conventionally pretty, young pop stars or models… rather than the older comedians, politicians or journalists who made up the male part of the show. If I needed anything to spell out to me that women were being judged for how old they were and what they looked like (rather than how witty and interesting they were), then this was it.

Something needed to change. And it changed on Twitter… where in January 2012 an online conversation with a range of people about the lack of visibility of women comedians led me to impetuously say, "Well, I shall just put a comedy night on myself!" Something I instantly felt doubt about – largely because I'd never previously organised anything bigger than my wedding.

Like all the best feminist initiatives, what became What The Frock! was a team effort. While it was me who led it and drove it and did the bulk of the graft, there was a huge network of people (many of whom I met on Twitter, before later meeting them in real life) who helped me to get the first night off the ground, and many more who have helped since. Some stalwarts, such as Gaby and Emily, have been here since day one. They're truly brilliant people.

By coincidence, What The Frock! was born into the same era of pop culture that also produced such positive forces for feminist energy as the No More Page 3 campaign and the Everyday Sexism Project, which have really captured the nation's attention and mobilised a new generation of feminists. I'm not suggesting that What The Frock! carries the same gravitas, but I am suggesting that the time was evidently ripe for women to stand up and stop accepting all this patriarchal bullshit society was throwing at them.

INVISIBILITY

Just as women in public spaces are subjected to catcalls, street harassment and unwanted and intimidating attention, the same applies in comedy clubs. All too often, comedians tell me of their experiences at other clubs – where they have been the token woman on the bill – and the male compere will introduce them as "the woman comedian" with a note of apology in his voice, which can be easily translated as "sorry, but this is your chance to go for a slash and get a drink". Researcher Yael Kohen quotes American stand-up Paula Poundstone recalling how the crowd at a club had gone wild for a male comedian's crude jokes before the compere comes back on to introduce her saying: "All right, the fun time's over. And now, please welcome Paula Poundstone [2]."

Similarly, the kind of heckles directed at women comedians are ones that would never be hurled at a man – the "Get your tits out", "Tell us a joke" and "Go back to the kitchen and make us a sandwich, love" kind of inspired genius. The heckles thrown at women in mixed gender comedy clubs are those intended to put them in their place, while those hurled at male comedians often reassert his sexual dominance or power. Heckles aimed at women tend to remind us that she is a sexual object, someone who is judged first by her appearance, while those aimed at men are more matey and conspiratorial.

In early 2014, a fair bit of attention was given to the fact that many clubs have a one-woman-only policy. This isn't news to anyone in the industry and I've heard countless tales from acts who tell me they're miffed that they've just been axed or rejected from a line-up as "they've already got a woman on that night" or had a woman on the previous month and "she didn't go down very well". But in March 2014, comedian Jenny Collier made headlines around the UK after she Tweeted a screengrab of an email from a booker cancelling her gig because "the venue have decided they don't want too many women on the bill". The Tweet went viral and got people talking yet again about the lack of women on the circuit. Writing in *The Independent*, Jenny said: "This insinuates that female comics are somehow a separate genre, the sort of act that you either like or don't like [3]."

But this was nothing new. Janeane Garofalo recalls of the early 1990s: "Club owners would actually have the nerve to say … 'Well, we just had a female comic last weekend headlining and she bombed, so we're not going to have any more women.' … The first few times it happened I was shocked. Then I would say, 'Do you say, 'We had a white man here?' [4]."

Later on in 2014, various huge comedy festivals came under fire for having failed to book any women at all at their events. Just read that sentence again: they did not book any women comedians *at all*… for a comedy festival! Again the line came back that none of the women they asked were available. Which is staggering. It's staggering that they were so short-sighted as to think that nobody would notice there were no women; it's staggering that none of the male comedians booked thought to question the testosterone-fuelled bill; it's staggering that the sponsors of those festivals didn't think twice about the fact they were slashing their potential audience reach in two. It's just staggering in the 21st Century that this is still even a topic for conversation.

Or is it? After all, it was only as recently as 1928 that women over 21 were granted the right to vote on the same terms as men. And it was even more recently in 1948 that women were finally allowed to sit their exams and graduate from Cambridge University. And yet more recently in 1984 that female athletes were permitted to run the marathon race in the Olympic Games (there was a genuine fear, I kid you not, that running for an extended period of time would cause their wombs to fall out). Actually, put into context… maybe it's not so staggering that festival and gig organisers don't realise they're not booking women until somebody points it out to them. In 2013, the Bank of England was prepared to issue a whole series of bank notes with not one solitary woman on until an internet campaign was launched to have at least one woman represented across the four notes. Women are still invisible to society. We have to make a lot of noise before people see us. And then they tell us off for not being ladylike.

While comedy is of course subjective, I think we can agree that of the endless male comedians doing the rounds, many of them simply aren't very funny. So are they there just because it's safer to have an unfunny man than a funny woman? Are comedy bookers and TV producers threatened by intelligent and witty women, so much so that it's easier to book Russell Howard or Rob Beckett again and hope for the best? Of course, there are plenty of women who aren't very funny. But why not ditch some of the unfunny men and replace them with some of the women who actually are funny? That seems easy to do. And thanks to the ongoing gender pay gap women won't cost as much, so everyone's a winner! (*NB: this is an attempt at satire.*)

QUOTAS

As Lucy Porter mentions in her foreword, the BBC's Director of Television Danny Cohen infamously announced in February 2014 that the station was introducing a policy of insisting there be at least one woman on all its radio and TV panel shows. While this was a well-intentioned move and one that was long overdue, perhaps it could have been handled differently. By going public with this headline statement, it looked like Danny wanted applause for being a hero and rescuing the poor women from the comedy gutter. A better move would have been to quietly issue a memo to all bookers and programmers in his corporation, and for the change to happen without fanfare. This would have been a far less patronising way of starting to remedy the problem.

But the problem – and it *is* a problem – is more widespread than just being a case of *Mock The Week* rarely having a female guest. Consider the language used to describe female performers and that used to talk about their male peers. For instance, skimming through the scrapbooks of What The Frock! cuttings, I see a bizarre range of terms used to describe the women who perform with us: "funny gals", "funny-maker", "sweetly demeanoured", "warm and chatty", "sweet voiced", "amiable and chatty banter" and so on. And I'm forever baffled by the genre of "female comedy" that What The Frock! is often billed as promoting. While the language used to write about one of the world's most successful contemporary female comedians – Sarah Silverman – is even more extraordinary: she's "adorable", she's "babelicious", she's "sexy"…

These are phrases to imply maternal hugs, bland giggles or sexy fun times. There was an interview with award-winning political comedian Bridget Christie in the December 2013 issue of *Vogue* with the headline "Pretty Funny". Not only would that headline never go with a piece about a male comedian, but it also implies that Bridget's appearance is somehow relevant, that it is surprising that she should be amusing, and that she is simply only a little bit funny. What with her being a lady person, a wife and a mother. Imagine the same headline on an interview with, for example, Bridget's husband: political comedian Stewart Lee.

The othering of women's comedy as a genre all of it's own (which it isn't, by the way) continues even today – and I acknowledge that all-female nights such as What The Frock! are not entirely helpful in this respect. But there is often the misconception by outsiders that women performing comedy are doing so in a way that will alienate men, that the jokes will be at the man's expense, and that ultimately the gags will be feminist and angry. I can think of hardly any women who fit this description.

One UK comedy festival proudly states on its website that alongside hosting some of the very best comedians on the circuit, it will also have shows by "children, women and disabled performers" [5]. Honestly! I realise it is said with the best of intentions, but by grouping women together with an actual minority group such as disabled people, then as women we really do have a long way to go. We make up 51% of the population! However, if we are going to be classed as a minority, I think the least we deserve is special parking bays and reduced price cinema tickets as compensation.

This problem with language usage leads me to another pet hate – the word 'comedienne'. It's seemingly only a little thing, but the use of the word 'comedienne' to describe a woman who makes people laugh really grates. It implies that the word 'comedian' is male and therefore superior, so anything else is a poor substitute. It implies a sense of otherness with a female comedian, a sense of second best, it gives a hint of frailty and suggests that a woman telling jokes is somehow different to a man telling jokes. Which is balls.

Because I make a deliberate gender distinction in my booking policy, I inevitably spend a lot of time reading cuttings about the acts who perform with What The Frock! that refer to them as 'comediennes'. Now don't get me wrong – I am delighted when anybody writes anything at all about my events. But given the opportunity, I do find myself saying to journalists who contact me: "I don't want to be annoying, and I'm not going to ask to approve the copy… but please call the acts 'comedians' and not 'comediennes'. It's about what comes out of their mouth not what their mouth looks like."

On the whole, they do listen and sometimes it leads to an interesting debate. One such male journalist who I had this debate with, and who subsequently amended his ways, wrote a piece this January in which he again referred to a woman as a 'comedienne'. I sent him in an email gently teasing him for this, in the light of the fact we'd discussed it several times before. He replied: "You're right re 'comedienne'. Ouch. That word now slips in to my writing subconsciously, frozen into my vocab from less enlightened times on [magazine title removed] when it sounded playful. We were neologisms-a-go-go back then. How do I flush it out of my writing? *Semper vigilans.*" So yeah, we're making progress!

You don't get the same gender distinction in most other professions. You don't get male dentists and female dentistas; you don't get male lawyers and female lawyerettes; you don't get male accountants and female sumsticians. For one thing, they're all really ugly words. For another thing, they're all made-up words.

Back in the 1920s when the first wave of women was permitted to graduate from some universities in the UK, they were not called 'graduates' like the men were. No. They were called 'graduettes'. I kid you not. Understandably these hard-working and fiercely intelligent women objected so strongly to this grossly patronising and condescending term that it has dropped out of use. Good for them.

Every single one of the 150+ acts I've worked with to date refers to herself as a 'comedian'. Some make a point of saying they actively distance themselves from the word 'comedienne', while others say they don't like the word but they'd rather somebody wrote something about them than nothing at all.

I know there are bigger things to worry about, but when we are still giving a job title different words depending on the gender of the person doing it, we need to think about how much further we have to go in the equality battle. And if people keep on calling them 'comediennes' rather than 'comedians', things aren't going to change any time soon. I'm not for a second implying this is the only problem women in the comedy industry are facing. But the nuances implied by a distinctively lesser word, one that is feminine and dainty in its sound and appearance, suggest that a gurl comedian is going to be a disappointment. When that's just poppycock.

This ties in to the problem of the kind of language that women are 'allowed' to use in comedy, compared to the language men are 'allowed' to use. For instance, it's considered OK for male comedians to use words like 'penis', 'balls', 'rape' and 'fuck' with no comeback. But if a female comedian uses words like 'vagina', 'labia' or 'vulva', well, she's deemed to be deliberately shocking. Perhaps this is because women are still supposed to be delicate creatures that politely look after the home, while still being available for a man's sexual fun… women are not supposed to be thinking human beings, and certainly not ones that leak.

One male journalist, who had just interviewed me for a piece about What The Frock! and why it existed, rejected my offer of free tickets to our next show. I asked why he didn't want to come. He said he wasn't sure if he'd like it. So I suggested he come anyway and if he didn't like it he could always leave and it wasn't like he'd have lost any money. He remained unconvinced… but after a short pause he asked me, in a curious tone: "So what happens at a women's comedy night?" It was like he thought we all sat on the floor in a big circle, holding hands and chanting to the goddess of menstruation (that's Mama Killa, by the way). I asked him if he'd ever been to a comedy club. "Oh yes," he said enthusiastically, "I love going to comedy clubs." I shrugged and said: "Well, it's like that. It's just a comedy club." I left him a pair of tickets on the door but he never showed up.

There seems to be a fear of what a female comedy night entails. I've read many pieces about What The Frock! where the male writer seems to be wanting some kind of medal for having "braved" the women in order to attend. And then they always – ALWAYS – write about how it wasn't as terrifying as they feared, and that they "genuinely" laughed. While this is great news, it's also depressing that they had these thoughts in the first place.

POWER GAMES

What comes up time and again when reading and talking around the issue of women in comedy is the topic of power. Who has it, who wants it, and who doesn't want anyone else to have it?

When I interviewed her in January 2012, comedian Kate Smurthwaite said: "If the clubs book lots of male acts doing sexist material, then they'll attract audiences who appreciate that. Comedy does become something that is generally perceived as by and for men. It's tough to challenge that: clubs will lose audiences in the short term if they buck the trend, but in the long term they'll benefit because more women will want to come and there'll be more variety among the acts and more great talent to choose from. I think, to be honest, some of the guys currently doing well are very, very afraid of clubs booking more women because they're not sure they'll be able to compete [6]."

There are two aspects to the power debate when it comes to women and comedy – firstly, there seems to be some concern about whether it is feminine for women to be the clowns, and secondly there are issues about what kind of merry hell might be unleashed on the world if the wims are proven to be just as funny as – or, gasp, more funny than – the menz. I say all this with tongue very much in cheek, obviously. LOL.

More seriously, there are some fantastic women out there who take clowning to extremes. Slapstick comedian Mabel Normand wasn't afraid to take a custard pie in the face. And Miranda Hart has got clowning down to a fine art. She is brilliant at physical slapstick humour and refusing to take herself seriously. What The Frock!'s resident compere Jayde Adams is the finest clown I've ever seen – a woman who uses her physical appearance to incite humour, and to confront audience expectations of what a woman of her larger size might be capable of. Jayde hosted the night's first birthday party while literally dressed as a clown.

The language used to describe a comedy performance is also aggressive. If an act does well, they 'killed', and if they didn't do well, they 'bombed'. Yael Kohen makes a joke of this in the title of her 2012 book celebrating the rise of women in American comedy, *We Killed*, while journalist and comedian Viv Groksop runs a night in the UK called *The Night I Died* – which uses the chat show format to invite a series of performers to hilariously reminisce about their worst ever experiences on stage.

It seems dated to contemporary audiences brought up in more enlightened times, but there is still a small market for sexist humour or jokes that make light of rape. Whether or not the intention of those jokes is to grab headlines or to remind women of their place, the fact that audiences keep turning up to see these acts is extraordinary and depressing.

Sarah Silverman is known for making jokes about rape in her stand-up sets, and it's hard to decide whether her material causes controversy because of its content or because its delivered by an attractive woman who blends vulgarity with vulnerability. But if you listen to the routine in question [7], Sarah is actually subverting the idea that rape survivors are to blame for being attacked and she is putting the power back in their hands. On the other hand, when male comedian Mike Sheer wrote an article on the UK comedy industry website Chortle in 2012 concluding that "women are less funny than rape" [8], it was deemed OK because he was a man saying it. Mike's article rightly attracted a lot of angry feedback and he responded by claiming it was satire. In effect: it was just a joke, can't you take a joke? It's just 'banter': a word that is now so bastardised by sexist lad-culture that it has no positive connotations whatsoever.

Is Sarah Silverman shocking because she is talking about a horrific subject and because she is seemingly making a joke of it, or because she is talking about something that nice girls just don't mention? Ie rape, sex, anything about the, y'know, downstairs area? Why is it OK for male comedians to talk about their wangs, blow jobs and to offer tips for cheating on your girlfriend... but not for women to do the same? As Susan Horowitz writes: "Female comics are expected to go further than civilian funny women – but not too far [9]."

Sarah shocks audiences in the 2000s with her coarse language and explicit subject matter, but really she's not doing anything different to male acts such as Lenny Bruce or Richard Pryor in the 1960s, 1970s and 1980s. Even in 2013, when Seth MacFarlane hosted the Academy Awards and did so with a series of offensive, cruel and controversial jibes at other people's expense, it was dismissed as just comedy. If a female host had done what Seth did, there is no way her career would have recovered in the way that Seth's effortlessly bounced back.

Another excuse offered for why women are less prominent on the comedy circuit (and this excuse is only offered by men) is that they are less suited to it, owing to wanting to be at home with their children. Wow! What about the many touring male comedians who also have kids waiting for them at home? Nobody thinks they're lesser parents for being away on tour. At a 2014 business symposium in Bristol, power player Karren Brady responded to an audience question about how she juggled motherhood with running her businesses saying simply: "I have a uterus and a brain and I'm capable of using both at the same time." You got the feeling it wasn't the first time she'd said it.

GENRE DEFINING

Initially, I hoped to get through this entire book without making reference to *that* silly little Christopher Hitchens article in *Vanity Fair* [10], but in hindsight to have done so would be pretending that such ignorant points of view don't persist. Christopher titled his 2007 piece 'Why Women Aren't Funny' in a deliberate attempt to ruffle feathers. Boringly, he succeeded. The thrust of his article was that women didn't need to be funny because men don't find funny women attractive. The implication being that the sole raison d'etre for a woman is to attract a mate. Like we're cavewomen and we must breed or else. Although with singles ads repeatedly stating that the mate being advertised for must possess a good sense of humour, one might beg to differ with Christopher – men evidently *do* find funny women attractive. Or do their adverts mean they only want a woman to laugh at the jokes made by the man? Boy, dating is a complicated minefield.

Christopher resorted to the old anti-feminist tactic of pitching 'pretty' women against 'ugly' women, with the implication that 'pretty' women neither needed to be, nor were capable of being, funny – while 'ugly' women *could* be funny but only because they had so little else going for them. It spawned hundreds of angry articles and is best left in the bigoted dustbin of history. American comedian Zane Busby concurs in Yael Kohen's book: "There were very few [women] in history who were ever considered beautiful, ladylike and funny. Because beauty isn't funny [11]."

In her autobiography *Bossypants*, the brilliant comedian Tina Fey offers the best possible response to Hitchens and his ilk: "We don't fucking care if you don't like it... I don't like Chinese food, but I don't write articles trying to prove that it doesn't exist [12]."

Of course, not all contemporary female performers identify as feminists but it's safe to say that more do than don't. Nadia Kamil's feminist burlesque routine became an online viral hit in early 2014 [13], Bridget Christie won the Foster's award at Edinburgh 2013 with an explicitly feminist show performed in a No More Page 3 campaign t-shirt; and all-female comedy events such as What The Frock! are seeing a rise in audiences, performers and media attention. The time is ripe for change.

CHAPTER THREE

Who were the women?

"Measured by ordinary standards of humour, she is about as comical as a crutch... A woman was made to be loved and fondled. She was certainly not made to be laughed at."
1909 newspaper report [14]

What's funny to one person is unbearably tedious to another, it's all subjective. But what *is* comedy? In it's simplest definition, the *Oxford English Dictionary* says comedy is a "stage play of light and amusing character". But comedy is not confined to a theatre or a genre. Comedy can be sung, it can be written, it can be spoken... it can be implied in a facial expression or a tone of voice. Comedy can be performed by anyone and interpreted by anyone else. It can be used to entertain, to educate, to inform or to amuse. It can be used to win power... or deflect power. But, as the *Oxford English Dictionary* says, at its most base level comedy is amusing. If comedy doesn't amuse you, it's failed.

The roots of comedy extend back into the roots of all written history. According to academic Matthew Bevis, "the institutional birth date for comedy is 486 BC, when space was made for it in the dramatic competitions at the festivals in Athens in honour of Dionysus [15]."

Greek philosopher Socrates observed that comedy was not confined to the stage but to "the greater stage of human life". He added that one of the joys of watching comedy is watching others play the buffoon while we ourselves are too inhibited to do so. Aristophanes was a renowned comic playwright and director who is frequently cited as the father of comedy. He understood the power of using tragedy to make comedy and his work is still taught and performed today.

Aristotle observed that "a joke is a form of abuse" [16] and again, little seems to have changed in the past few millennia. However, the get-out-of-jail-free card of saying "It's just a joke" – or worse, "It's only banter" – is generally accepted as an excuse for an insult by someone too unimaginative to come up with something intelligent to say.

As early as 1885 there was a book published to attempt to refute the nonsense idea that women were not funny. Kate Sanborn's *The Wit Of Women* was an anthology of funny women that was written solely to demonstrate that the ladies do indeed have a sense of humour. A subsequent attempt at hammering home the point came in 1934 via Martha Bensley Bruère and Mary Ritter Beard's anthology *Laughing Their Way: Women's Humor in America*. The only thing that is depressing about the existence of these two books is that it highlights just how very long we've been trying to prove that women do the funnies as well as the men do... and clearly we still have a long way to go. I'm writing this book almost 130 years after Kate's book was published, and the fact I need to do this is enough to make a grown woman weep.

The big problem for women, especially in the early decades that we're looking at here, is that there is no tradition of women being the ones telling the jokes, while there is a long history of men in comedy roles – whether as court jesters, music hall heroes, slapstick movie stars or stand-ups selling out arena tours. But with the few women who did enter those professions often either dressing as men or adopting a male pseudonym in order to be accepted, it's clear to see how hard the ensuing generations of funny women need to work in order to be taken seriously as comedians. NB: this isn't exclusive to comedy but to every single profession.

THE 1900s AND 1910s

When it comes to women, where do you start? To my mind, the roots of our current stand-up comedy circuit hail from the British tradition of music hall, which boomed from the mid-19th to mid-20th Centuries and introduced us to such wonderful character performers as Marie Lloyd (1870-1922) and Vesta Tilley (1864-1952).

In a pre-cinema era, music halls welcomed varied entertainment including song, dance, vaudeville, cabaret and more to its stages, often in ornate, Victorian theatres. Wilton's Music Hall in East London remains the world's oldest and still functioning music hall, while the Malt Cross in Nottingham has been beautifully restored to show contemporary audiences exactly how stunning music halls could be.

Although initially attracting a mostly male and working-class clientele, music hall impresario Charles Morton swept onto the scene in the 1850s and opened the first purpose-built music hall… one which deliberately catered to what Charles felt were the requirements of not only the middle classes but also of women. And the Canterbury Arms in Lambeth was his first example of this, where he would decorate the theatre in a stunning manner, display fine art on the walls and hold, for instance, ladies' evenings on Thursdays. Music halls were not seen as particularly respectable places but by slowly including isolated ladies' evenings, women began to come to the music halls until it became as acceptable for women to enjoy the shows as for men to.

In terms of the performers, while men dominated the music hall stages there were still a good number of phenomenally popular women. The most successful women performers developed a sophisticated humour based on the preoccupations of their audiences, which meant that (just as today) their routines were dominated by drink, marriage, money worries and social status. For instance, Maidey Scott's song *I'm Glad I Took My Mother's Advice* was typical of the mildly suggestive material that played on the Victorian fears of moral turpitude – with it's lines about never kissing the boys (so she lets them kiss her), and never climbing trees with boys (instead they stand beneath and look up her skirts).

Bessie Bellwood (1856-1896), who'd started life as a rough and ready rabbit skinner near London's Waterloo Station, had a song called *What Cheer Ria*, about a market stall holder who'd treated herself to a seat in the opulent music hall stalls (rather than the bare balcony, which was more befitting of her status) and the calamity and social embarrassment that ensued – the moral of the tale being: Bessie, know your place!

Bessie had a reputation for flattening hecklers and in 1892 novelist Jerome K Jerome describes seeing her rebut a man who dared to shout back. In a lengthy description of the event, Jerome recalls how Bessie spent more than five minutes delivering such scathing and belittling put downs to the heckler that by the time she had finished, the entire music hall erupted in a standing ovation. Go, Bessie!

The women in music hall tended to draw on their personal experiences more than the men did, but another tactic was to play the men at their own game – as Vesta Tilley did by performing as a male impersonator. At the time, a woman dressed as a man was generally considered shocking, but the music hall was one place where it was accepted. Vesta is now the best-remembered male impersonator from the music halls. While male performers might strut on stage and sing songs about being drunk and the number of women they'd 'mashed', male impersonators such as Vesta had more boyish characters, ones who were much less threatening and more romantic towards the audience.

During the First World War, male impersonators really came into their own, turning out in military uniform to rally the troops. Vesta became affectionately known as 'Britain's best recruiting sergeant'. But when the war was over the culture of music halls had changed... along with everything else in the UK.

Over in the States, it was a similar story. They may not have had music halls as such but they did have concert saloons. The saloons provided entertainment by men for men, with women allowed in as waiters (and doubling up as prostitutes). As such, the saloons inevitably didn't tend to attract a respectable class of customer. By the 1850s, the saloons were including comedy, acrobatics, music and dancing on their bills... with women only permitted to perform as barely-dressed dancers. How was a woman with aspirations beyond being a can-can dancer supposed to make a name for herself in that kind of environment?

In 1860, in an attempt to curb the level of prostitution in concert saloons, a law was passed in New York prohibiting women from working as waiters in the saloons. This meant that the saloon managers needed to find a new way to bring attractive women into the club for the entertainment of the male audience. The answer was to allow women to perform in the new 'variety theatres' as the saloons became known. The expectation was still that women would be skimpily dressed dancers and that they would flirt with the male customers, but as time progressed women slowly started to be the sidekicks in male comedy acts. By the 1890s a few female comedians in the US were making a name as solo acts, such as Beatrice Herford (1868-1952) – who wrote and performed her own material, and who counted the satirist Dorothy Parker among her fans. Another success story was Ruth Draper (1884-1956), who performed popular comedy sketches.

As time went on, more and more women were becoming draws in their own right in the variety theatres. Sophie Tucker and Mae West were just two names that could bring in the crowds. Mae famously progressed from the vaudeville stage to the Broadway stage with relative ease, and by the 1930s she had become a Hollywood film star – despite being the (now unheard of) age of 40 when she made her very first feature film *Night After Night* (1932).

THE 1920s and 1930s

Cinema had begun to boom during the war years as a cheap means of escapism, and while early cinema was shown in music halls alongside variety acts it wasn't long before the movies took over as a viable night out on their own terms.

In the era of the flickering silver screen, a new type of funny woman was starting to emerge – whether she was a silent ingénue along the lines of Constance Talmadge (1898-1973) and Marion Davies (1897-1961) – or an all-singing all-dancing diva à la Marilyn Monroe (1926-1962) or Ginger Rogers (1911-1995). Finally given voices, the stars of the cinema were able to move away from physical slapstick to more subtle spoken comedy.

Some music hall stars (such as Charlie Chaplin, Stan Laurel, Betty Balfour and Mabel Normand) made the move successfully from the music hall stage to the silent screen, but many fell by the wayside and were soon forgotten by fickle audiences.

One star who survived the move from music halls to the cinema screen was Marie Dressler (1868-1934), who played on being a big, bulky and gawky-looking woman. At one point in the 1930s, Marie was an even bigger audience draw than the more conventionally attractive Greta Garbo. Marie's comedy was coarse and vulgar but always performed with dignity. One of her contemporaries who made a similar success out of being an 'ugly duckling' was Fanny Brice (1891-1951), who had a routine about being a fan dancer stumbling her way through a terrible version of *The Dying Swan*: which was aped to perfection in a 1952 episode of Lucille Ball's TV sitcom *I Love Lucy*.

THE 1940s

The screwball comedies of the 1930s and 1940s were a prime opportunity for women. Performers such as Claudette Colbert (1903-1996), Carole Lombard (1908-1942), Myrna Loy (1905-1993) and Rosalind Russell (1907-1976) excelled as the fast-talking dames positioned as romantic leads in these sexy comedies. Rosalind's portrayal of brilliant journalist Hildy Johnson in *His Girl Friday* (1940) is a perfect example – as she runs rings around the men who are always one step behind her but persistently wanting to get in her knickers.

Multi-award winning Carol Channing (1921-), who played Lorelei Lee in the 1949 stage version of *Gentlemen Prefer Blondes* (a comedy written by the brilliant Anita Loos), was known for her malapropisms, such as "Possession is twelve tenths of the law". She was deliberately playing up to the dumb blonde stereotype, even though this was far from her reality as a graduate: she knew it was what audiences expected of a beautiful woman.

But even though women had started to make a name for themselves as character performers in the music halls and concert saloons, or on the silent and talking cinema screens... the world of stand-up was still relatively untapped territory. It was an emerging market for both men and women, and in the 1940s comedy was on the cusp of taking the shape we now recognise as the stand-up circuit. This was a result of the nightclub culture that evolved during the wars. In the post-World War Two era, stand-up was dominated by men. The very business of standing up in front of a group of people and asserting your authority as the person to be listened to demanded a lot of power... and audiences were not yet ready to give that power to women. For a woman to stand behind a microphone and make a room full of people laugh would be for a woman to undo her femininity.

Another area where funny women were excelling was in literature. Dodie Smith (1896-1990), for instance, published the endearing novel *I Capture The Castle* in 1940; and the comic tragedy *The Pursuit Of Love* was published by Nancy Mitford (1904-1973) in 1945. These were following in the tradition of Stella Gibbons' (1902-1989) romantic parody *Cold Comfort Farm*, which has been lapped up by rapturous readers since 1932. And while we're on the subject of witty women writers, let's not forget Jane Austen (1775-1817) who made a career out of wise and witty satirical parodies that are still read and adored today.

Making a break for radio freedom was Hattie Jacques (1922-1980), who progressed from the theatrical stage to radio drama in the 1940s on shows such as *It's That Man Again*, before becoming one of Tony Hancock's sidekicks on *Hancock's Half Hour* in the 1950s and 1960s. At the same time, Hattie was also a series regular in the British *Carry On* franchise, which played on the bawdy humour popular from old-fashioned seaside postcards. Hattie was frequently cast in a matronly role, and the character of a hospital matron is still associated with her busty form. In 2011, Welsh comic actor Ruth Jones (1966-) portrayed Hattie in the eponymous BBC film *Hattie*, which was a fitting tribute to this comedy gem and remains the most-watched programme ever shown on BBC4.

THE 1950s

The rise of televisions in the home from the mid-1950s widened the scope for performers. Stand-up comedian Joan Rivers (1933-2014) graduated from the club circuit to being a TV performer on the US's popular *The Today Show* in the mid-1960s. Joan started out by performing in strip clubs, which in the 1950s was a regular home for male stand-ups… less so for female stand-ups. As you can imagine, the customers in strip clubs were less interested in anything the women might have to say and more interested in being served drinks and tits by them. But Joan cut her comedy teeth in strip clubs, performing under the name Pepper January (tagline 'Comedy with Spice'), yet she was frequently heckled and booed off stage by randy punters, bored by this fully clothed woman telling them jokes, and yelling "Bring on the girls" at her. So it's easy to see that if in the 1950s the main arena in which to hone your skills as a stand-up was in the strip clubs, then the funny women out there were already facing a disadvantage.

Meanwhile, June Whitfield (1925-) started out in radio comedies in the 1950s and has rarely been off our TVs ever since the 1960s thanks to shows such as *Hancock's Half Hour*, *Terry and June* and *Absolutely Fabulous*. In 2013, she was handed the Comedy Legend award by the annual Slapstick Festival.

Lucille Ball (1911-1989) became the star of five separate sitcoms that incorporated her name in the title, starting with *I Love Lucy* in 1951, showing the true power that her name was worth. The show repeatedly won Emmy awards as well as a host of other accolades, and was memorable not only for showing Lucille/Lucy in a mixed race marriage with her real-life Cuban husband Desi Arnaz, but also for pioneering the tactic of filming a sitcom in front of a live studio audience – something still regularly done today.

THE 1960s

In the post-war period of recovery, there was a move for women to give up the manual work they had undertaken during the war and go back to the kitchen. In 1961, journalist Siriol Hugh-Jones wrote a baffling feature for British magazine *The Twentieth Century* called 'We Witless Women' reporting on the widely held assumption that British women are "rarely witty". Despite being a woman herself, Siriol stated that a woman who *was* witty was someone to be suspicious of and compared such a woman to a 1920s' circus freak who would be kept behind bars and jeered at by passers by. She reassuringly concluded: "No need to alarm yourself, they're not all going to be like this." From this, it's safe to presume that Siriol wanted to make it clear that she herself had no sense of humour.

Following on from Hattie Jacques in the *Carry On* films, British actor Barbara Windsor (1937-) also became synonymous with the franchise – frequently cast as the naïve, giggly, blonde and buxom silly girl. Between 1964 and 1974, Barbara appeared in 10 *Carry On* films, and perhaps because of her association to the *Carry On* brand (which had a style of humour harking back to bawdy music hall humour) in 1970 Barbara was cast as music hall star Marie Lloyd in the biopic *Sing A Rude Song*. In a varied and busy career ever since, Barbara repeatedly returns to Christmas pantomimes – a theatre genre that itself owes a great debt to the music hall tradition.

Another US comedian who started in the strip clubs was Goldie Hawn (1945-), who in the 1960s was a go-go dancer before being spotted and cast in *Good Morning, World* and later *Rowan and Martin's Laugh In* – TV shows in which she giggled her way through roles as a bumbling blonde. Grateful for the career boost but unhappy about her dumb blonde persona or having to appear in bikinis (and for her body to be daubed in amusing slogans), Goldie worked hard to show what she was really worth as a performer. And by 1969, Goldie had proved her worth as a comedy actor in the film *Cactus Flower*, for which she won an Oscar and a lifelong career in Hollywood.

Roseanne Barr (1952-) also started out as a waiter but enjoyed the snarky put downs to her customers so much that she decided to try her luck behind the mic instead.

Over in the UK, Joyce Grenfell (1910-1979) rose to fame in the 1940s as a result of her role as a wartime entertainer, trying to keep the soldiers' spirits up. In the 1950s, Joyce worked as a writer on satirical comedies at the BBC before becoming a sidekick to other comedians in front of the camera. By the 1960s, Joyce was so popular that she was also performing in the States – including alongside Elvis Presley on *The Ed Sullivan Show*. But she is best remembered for her monologues and for her harassed nursery nurse character with her "Don't do that, George" catchphrase.

THE 1970s

"If it weren't for the women's movement, people would call it [comedy] my hobby."
Comedian Lily Tomlin

Even in the 1970s, in the age of women's liberation and an era that proudly made great leaps in the advancement of women's rights, it was still tough to be a funny woman. American comedy writer Deanne Stillman was submitting articles to the satirical *Mad* magazine under the pen name 'Dean' so that they would be accepted for print, and admits that as a teenager she thought that "writing funny was something girls didn't do [17]."

But women's liberation did make it easier for performers such as Bette Midler

(1945-) to progress as bawdy comedians with filthy jokes and unconventional looks. On a similar note, the 1970s also saw the puppet character Miss Piggy (1974-) make her debut as a regular character in *The Muppets* – she was the only recurring female Muppet. Piggy possessed ferocious sexual appetites and power to match those of Mae West or Roseanne Barr, and she did so while being a larger size and a glamorous man(frog)eater. Go, Piggy, and thank you for shaking up the idea of what a female romantic lead can look like.

Caroline Hirsch (1952-) still runs the famous Caroline's On Broadway comedy club in New York City that opened in 1982, and she credits the women's movement of the 1970s with giving women the impetus to really push themselves as stand-up comedians. All the great acts have passed through Caroline's doors – everyone from Jerry Seinfeld to Sandra Bernhard, Bill Hicks, Rosie O'Donnell and Kathy Griffin.

Victoria Wood (1953-) and Julie Walters (1950-) were a much-loved British double act who emerged in the 1970s, and went on to have hugely popular success together on TV in the 1980s. With the expansion of TV in the 1980s and the introduction of new terrestrial channels as well as satellite and cable TV stations, the opportunities for performers widened considerably as programmers started casting their nets ever wider to find new content.

Fawlty Towers remains one of the most well loved BBC sitcoms of all time, despite only running for two series (1975-1979). And while Connie Booth (1944-) is best remembered as frustrated chambermaid Polly, few people realise that she also co-wrote the series alongside her then-husband John Cleese. But her role in creating such a phenomenally popular series (one that only spawned 12 episodes, but 12 episodes that have endured for almost 40 years) should certainly not be underestimated.

THE 1980s

As a result of all of this, the 1980s was a prime time for the new wave of alternative comedy that saw performers such as Dawn French (1957-) and Jennifer Saunders (1958-) emerge alongside the likes of Ruby Wax (1953-), Tracey Ullman (1959-) and co.

In the States, Roseanne Barr was turning the concept of women's role in comedy on its head. A well-built, coarse, working-class woman, she'd paid her dues in the stand-up clubs before landing her own ABC sitcom *Roseanne* (1987-2004) – a loosely fictionalised account of her own life. If this wasn't an example of women calling the shots, then nothing was. Roseanne's portrayal of a chaotic home life – with a family struggling to hold down jobs and to make ends meet, with wayward children and a crass turn of phrase – was a gleeful two-fingered salute to the dated idea of a 1950s stay-at-home housewife with her waspy waist, silent children and perfect manners.

The 1980s and early 1990s was an interesting time, because women were still allowed to age on screen. Imagine a sitcom such as *The Golden Girls* being commissioned now. Picture the pitch meeting: a show about four sassy, single, sex-loving older women house-sharing in Miami. It would never happen! Yet the resulting show, which ran from 1985-1992, remains an enormously funny, sharp and considerate portrayal of female friendship and relationships in general. *The Golden Girls* didn't end due to a drop in ratings, but because cast member Bea Arthur decided she had had enough of the show.

In 1986, Joan Rivers became the first female host of a late-night talk show in the US with *The Late Show*, which ran until 1988. Also in 1986, Ellen DeGeneres (1958-) made history by being the first comedian to chat with talk show host Larry Carson at his desk after a set on the show. For such an influential man as Larry to make this invitation signalled to the US audiences that Ellen was a talent to take note of, and her career has continued to sky rocket ever since.

In 1983, a former journalist called Nora Ephron (1941-2012) published her wickedly comic novel *Heartburn,* inspired by her husband's infidelity. Nora went on to become enormously successful and respected for writing the scripts to many of Hollywood's finest romantic comedy films, including *When Harry Met Sally* (for which she won a BAFTA), *Sleepless In Seattle* and *You've Got Mail.*

THE 1990s

Returning to the theme of funny women novelists, there was a surge of new fiction in the 1990s that fitted the bill. This was the decade that introduced us to the haphazard diarist Bridget Jones, as created by Helen Fielding

(1958-) – a character who went on to feature in two further best-selling diaries, and who has been the subject of (to date) two Hollywood blockbusters. Around the same time, comic novels by the likes of Arabella Weir (1957-) and Meera Syal (1961-), alumni from *The Fast Show* and *Goodness Gracious Me* respectively, also appeared in bookshops. And these are just a few examples from a huge comic bookshelf.

On TV, the sitcom *Friends* (1994-2004) and comedy-drama *Sex And The City* (1998-2004) caught a new wave of interest for their female comedy leads. They were seen to portray young, independent women living in New York City, earning their own incomes, free from parental or spousal ties, and flitting from relationship to fling without (initially) a child at home to worry about. But the women in these shows were also agonisingly thin, impossibly beautiful, and caught up in the endless cycle of thinking that if only they could meet Mr Right then all would be well with the world. They were also all white. In the 10-year history of *Friends*, there was only one African-American recurring cast member: Aisha Tyler, who played Ross's girlfriend Charlie for nine episodes (the show ran for 236 episodes). *Sex And The City* had no recurrent black actors. Not one.

In 1999, Tina Fey (1970-) became the first female head writer on *Saturday Night Live* since its launch in 1975. As a result, the show soon also featured a number of other brilliant female writers and comedians including Amy Poehler (1971-), Maya Rudolph (1972-) and Rachel Dratch (1966-), and a stream of more feminist-infused comedy – which had no negative impact on ratings whatsoever. Tina later used her experiences at *Saturday Night Live* when writing her hit NBC sitcom *30 Rock* – which exposed the men's club atmosphere of a late night sketch show. Do you know what else Tina does that is considered unusual? She is a woman wearing glasses on TV. How many other women can you think of who wear glasses on TV? Not many, huh? Not unless they're portraying a brainy, but unattractive, woman. As a result, Tina is often said to be touting "sexy librarian chic". Imagine the same being said about a man on TV who wears glasses.

The same men's club atmosphere was also satirised on *The Larry Sanders Show*, a sitcom based at a fictional late night talk show, when Sarah Silverman's (1970-) character Wendy was hired in season five (1997) as the token woman writer. Wendy's jokes were never used when she submitted them herself... however when she submitted them anonymously, they were used and considered hilarious. Ultimately, head scriptwriter Phil has to admit that he feels uncomfortable and threatened by a funny woman on his team. This echood Sarah's real-life experiences on *Saturday Night Live* as a writer in the 1993-1994 season when her jokes were persistently not used on air. Sarah's colleague on *The Larry Sanders Show*, Janeane Garofalo (1964-), was also a former *Saturday Night Live* writer (1994-1995 season) who left after only six months and complained of the sexist attitude.

THE 2000s

"There's so many funny women out there, and to be able to have a movie that has a lot of funny roles for women was so, so gratifying."
Kristin Wiig talking about *Bridesmaids*

Even in the 2000s' wave of female-led US comedy series (*2 Broke Girls*, *Parks and Recreation*, *Girls* etc), there is still a dearth of non-white women. Mindy Kaling's (1979-) *The Mindy Project* is a notable exception. And Issa Rae's (1985-) *The Mis-Adventures of Awkward Black Girl* has been a popular and award-winning web comedy series since 2011. While Wanda Sykes' (1964-) full-length comedy specials *I'ma Be Me* enjoy huge audiences on HBO. What's significant about Wanda's show is that she is not only black but also a lesbian. Even the title *I'ma Be Me* links to a dialect specific to African American audiences.

Former *Seinfeld* star Julia Louis-Deyfus (1961-) is now heading up the HBO political sitcom *Veep*; Lena Dunham (1986-) is winning awards and applause left, right and centre for her hit US show *Girls;* Sarah Millican (1975-) is selling out national tours in the UK and heading up her own regular BBC TV show; Miranda Hart (1972-) is filling arenas with comedy fans on the back of her phenomenally successful BBC sitcom; feminist comedian Bridget Christie (1971-) is selling out run after run in London's West End and packing out venues nationwide; relative newcomer Luisa Omielan (1982-) has sold out an astonishing five runs at London's Soho Theatre (to date) with her first two solo shows *What Would Beyonce Do?* and *Am I Right, Ladies?*; a new generation of Maggie Smith (1934-) fans on both sides of the Atlantic are hailing her a comedy legend for her priceless comic timing as the Dowager Countess in *Downton Abbey...*

Tina Fey's hit NBC sitcom *30 Rock* is a great example of a female led comedy show with feminist undertones, yet Tina is sometimes criticised for not having written every episode herself. Even though she was involved in the creation and production of every episode as well as being the star of every episode. She really can't win. However, in 2004, Tina wrote the script for the hit Lindsay Lohan film *Mean Girls*, which exposed the plasticised bullies at a high school for how shallow and hateful they were and did so with a wealth of comic punches.

In 2008, *The New York Times Book Review* decided to name its favourite funny novels of all time [18]. The results were a little depressing… since they included not one novel by a woman. Marian Keyes (1963-) and Carrie Fisher (1956-) might have something to say about this, as might Helen Fielding, Meera Syal, Stella Gibbons, Jane Austen and all the other witty women writers mentioned previously (and even more who have not yet been mentioned here).

The 2011 film *Bridesmaids* was responsible for rocking the boat and proving just how funny women really could be when permitted to play the boys at their own game. In a female-led cast (spearheaded by *Saturday Night Live* alumni Kristen Wiig and Maya Rudoph), and with a script written by Kristin Wiig and Annie Mumolo, *Bridesmaids* brought in almost $300 million at the box office and had audiences in stitches of laughter at gross-out gags, self-deprecating humour and send-ups of a grotesquely shallow boyfriend.

CHAPTER FOUR

Ahh! Here are the women!

Note: The selection of the 71 women was influenced by an online survey we carried out in 2012, from which more than 500 female comedians were nominated as the nation's favourites. These have been whittled down to try and encompass all genres (eg stand-up, literature, music hall, acting etc). In addition, the invited contributors have chosen the funny woman who most stands out to them personally. There will be women who you think have been foolishly excluded and others who you think should definitely not have been included, but it would have been impossible to please all readers. However, we invite you to find us on Twitter (@WTFrock_Comedy, with the hashtag #WTFBook) and Facebook (facebook.com/WhatTheFrockComedy) and join the discussion there. Let's celebrate as many funny women as humanly possible.

CAROLINE AHERNE (1963-)

Caroline Aherne is best known as a character act. She started out on the comedy circuit in the late 1980s as a comedy country and western act called The Mitzi Goldberg Experience, before graduating to radio where she developed the Mrs Merton character. Mrs Merton was a mock-naïve granny who hosted a BBC TV talk show for five series between 1995 and 1998. An ill-advised decision to relocate the production of the show from Manchester to Las Vegas in 1997 in order to attract big Hollywood stars as guests proved to be fatal for *The Mrs Merton Show*, and despite returning to the UK for the final show it was too late to save the format.

Alongside Mrs Merton, Caroline had also been a writer and performer in the BBC's hit comedy sketch show *The Fast Show*. However, Caroline and one of her *Mrs Merton* co-writers Craig Cash kept on working together, creating the multiple BAFTA-award winning sitcom *The Royle Family* in 1998. Caroline and Craig both wrote and starred in the hit show, which was largely set in the living room of a TV-obsessed Manchester family. *The Royle Family* attracted an illustrious cast that also included Sue Johnston, Ricky Tomlinson, Jessica Hynes and Liz Smith.

Since the early 2000s, Caroline has kept a low profile, preferring to write material for other performers and only appearing as an actor in a few specials of *The Royle Family*.

JENNIFER ANISTON (1969-)

From the moment she hit our TV screens in 1994 as spoilt princess Rachel Green in *Friends*, Jennifer Aniston cemented her place as a fantastic comedy actor. Through ten series of *Friends*, we saw Jennifer's performance make Rachel such a beloved character that she still has a hairstyle named after her. Jennifer owned the character so much that Rachel ended up with some of the funniest lines in the entire series – funny not only thanks to the writers but also to Jennifer's perfect comic timing.

Even before *Friends* ended in 2004, Jennifer had already been the only member of the cast to become a bonafide movie star in her own right... and she's carried on making films. OK, some of them are of dubious quality and many of them are somewhat sappy... but bear with me, because Jennifer has also made some sterling comedy films.

Check out *Office Space* (1999), in which she plays unfulfilled waiter Joanna, a workshy character who'd rather be sat at home watching telly. While Joanna is essentially a secondary character for the men to bounce off, in *Office Space* Jennifer suddenly came into her own as a comedy actress worth keeping an eye on.

But her standout comedy film role is as the titular Polly, alongside Ben Stiller, in *Along Came Polly* (2004) – in which she is a freewheeling, ferret-fancying loose cannon up against Ben's repressed suit. Even in *We're The Millers* (2013) – a film with an exemplary cast of comedy greats such as Jason Sudeikis, Nick Offerman and Scott Adsit – Jennifer owns her questionable role as a stripper-pretending-to-be-a-mom-on-a-family-holiday.

BEA ARTHUR (1922-2009)
By Chella Quint

I love Bea Arthur. What's not to love? A sex positive, intersectionally feminist, Jewish comedian from New York whose pet topics were women's health and minority identities, who championed LGBT rights and did AIDS activism in her spare time? Yes, please.

Growing up in the US in the late 1980s, I met her as Dorothy Zbornak on *The Golden Girls*, but much later I got to know her second wave feminist 1970s incarnation, *Maude*, while I was third waving it up and studying dramatic writing at NYU. Bea played strong roles throughout her career and had already been successful on Broadway but was most widely known for these two television sitcom characters, who both hilariously and poignantly broached taboo topics like abortion, contraception, menopause, gay relationships, ageism, feminism, politics and privilege (and that's just for starters) on primetime US terrestrial television across two decades.

On screen, she was never afraid to make a fool of herself, could clown and gurn with gracefully graceless precision. Bea's physical comedy was excellent but she was even funnier verbally. Some of my favourite lines on *The Golden Girls* were her perfectly delivered sarcastic comebacks, although she just as often created generous set ups for her castmates' punchlines: Bea was a real ensemble performer.

She could sing and dance, and her career started in theatre, which is every New York kid's dream. Even though she had trained in method acting with Lee Strasberg and had won a Tony award, her *Miami* duet in Dorothy's songwriting session with Rose seemed like the best use of her training – at least it did to me, as a little kid cracking up watching *The Golden Girls* at home on a Saturday night. Spoiler alert: in the episode, they're trying to win a competition and their song comes in second. I had suspended my belief so well that I remember turning to my parents, incredulous, demanding to know why their clearly brilliant song hadn't won first prize! My dad had to explain, chuckling, that there'd be no situation in the situation comedy if they'd actually won. My mom often shook her head and said, "This show is very adult", but she never made me leave the room or change the channel. It did lead to me asking precocious questions, like "what does inter-uterine mean"? I genuinely learned a lot from *The Golden Girls* and it was usually Dorothy's exasperated outbursts that clued me in to the more mature content.

Across all the roles she played, Bea was able to express anger with the perfect amount of clownish heightened reality that true rage is. Her 20-yard stare was notorious on and off screen. I can only dream of perfecting a withering gaze like hers.

Bea got her first big television role at age 50, and while it's amazing and perfect that she was a role model for older performers and an inspiration to all of us younger ones working hard at our craft, it's incredibly sad that we didn't get to see her on our screens for longer. Her parting gift? In her will, she donated $300,000 to New York's Ali Forney Center for Homeless LGBT Youth.

Bea totally paved the way for the kind of comedy I do now and want to do in the future. Nice one, Bea.

JANE AUSTEN (1775-1817)

By Andrew Hunter Murray

According to a distressingly large number of people – many of them men – there is nothing terribly interesting about Jane Austen. An old maid by 29, dead by 41, only wrote six books (not nearly as many as, say, James Paterson), almost exclusively about posh young women falling for posh young men. Bonnets feature heavily. American author and average talent Mark Twain said he wanted to dig her up and beat her over the head with her own shinbone.

Fortunately for us, Twain was wrong. Jane Austen was one of the most hilarious, waspish authors ever to grace the world of letters and could have dispatched Twain in six words had she wished. I first met Jane's work at a testosterone-y all-boys school at 16, an age when young men are largely unreceptive to anyone else's feelings, let alone those of dead middle-class Hampshire authoresses. So it was a bold English teacher who introduced us to her stuff. Dr McKeown, I owe you one.

Many years and multiple readings later, I have little sympathy with people who claim to dislike Jane, up to the point of offering to step outside and talk about it. The simple reason is that Jane is funny. Few writers could come up with a sharper one-liner than that dished out to Margaret Dashwood in *Sense and Sensibility*: '"I wish," said Margaret, striking out a novel thought, "that somebody would give us all a large fortune apiece!" Striking out a novel thought! Blink and you'd miss it. On the first couple of readings I did miss it. But what an elegant, stiletto-thin note of irony. Anyone who doesn't get that isn't reading closely enough or – entirely possible – doesn't have a sense of humour.

These days, 'Dear Jane' is everywhere – on TV, in the cinema, respectable enough even for the nation's banknotes. But as time goes by and the original novels are obscured by extra layers of adaptation and actresses (I'm looking at you, Gwyneth Paltrow), it's easy for Jane's jokes to go astray. Time places itself between her and us. William Shakespeare's jokes need to be delivered superbly to elicit a laugh today. The language barrier between us and Jane is smaller but it's there and growing; her sentences are more complex, her punchlines less accessible. And they're mostly by the narrator; remove Jane's tart observational eye and you end up with nothing but a starched, tedious comedy of manners. TV commissioners, please take note.

Yet the grotesque characters who spring off Jane's page rival any in *The Office* or *Frasier*, and their absurdities are all the funnier for their recognisability. Jane's cruelty shines forth as clearly as her wit: she knew that in comedy there are casualties. And while her humour swings back and forth between the genial and the savage, Jane's narrator almost never loses her lightness of touch or ability to laugh despite the threats of ruin or – worse – spinsterhood. So over to Jane herself for the closer: "Follies and nonsense, whims and inconsistencies do divert me, I own, and I laugh at them whenever I can." I am most grateful she did.

HYLDA BAKER (1905-1986)

Hylda Baker was that rare thing – a music hall performer who went on to find fame in films and on TV. As a 10-year-old, Hylda followed her father onto the stage of the music hall, and by the age of 14 she was writing and performing in her own shows which were loved for their daft catchphrases, such as "She knows, y'know" and "Be soon", which would become the title of her BBC television series in 1957.

Roles in several sitcoms soon followed, as well as more serious acting parts in films – including the seminal 1960 kitchen sink drama *Saturday Night and Sunday Morning* in which she played Aunt Ada. But it is her leading role in the 1968-1973 ITV sitcom *Nearest and Dearest* for which Hylda is best remembered. In this seven-season show she starred alongside comedian Jimmy Jewel, and the two played bickering middle-aged siblings who ran a business together.

Never one to do things by halves, Hylda lived her life like a true star – dressing in furs and keeping pet monkeys, proving that you really can take the girl out of Lancashire and there's definitely no going back.

BETTY BALFOUR (1903-1977)

British silent film star Betty Balfour was dubbed "the queen of happiness" thanks to her many comedy roles, most notably in the *Squibs* film series in the early 1920s. Her delicate looks and comic charm won the attention of producer George Pearson who championed Betty to make her film debut in 1920 with his comedy drama *Nothing Else Matters*. But George's *Squibs* series was where Betty really won her fans. Thanks to the four *Squibs* comedies, Betty became so popular that by the mid-1920s she was deemed one of the most famous people in Britain.

A misguided attempt to rebrand herself from the dippy Squibs persona led to a separation from George, and ultimately the beginning of the end. Although she went on to appear in an early Alfred Hitchcock film (the silent movie *Champagne*, 1928), like many silent stars Betty was to come unstuck with the dawning of the talkies and her career rapidly tailed off after the early 1930s.

LUCILLE BALL (1911-1989)
By Miranda Dawe

Lucille Ball was the first funny female I ever saw on screen; this beautiful but crazy lady would get into hilarious scrapes and pull funny faces with her big red lips and wide-eyes and I was mesmerised. Some of my earliest memories involve eating my lunch in front of *I Love Lucy* repeats: the show which lead me to be convinced that America was actually in black and white for more years than is sensible.

Lucille was certainly not as scatter-brained as her television alter ego Lucy Ricardo; she was a four-time Emmy winner and the first female head of a television studio. Life was not easy for Lucille – she had to work very hard to get to be a household name.

She had started her career as a model in New York before a debilitating bout of rheumatoid arthritis set her back two years. Once recovered, she worked in chorus roles on Broadway but continually got sacked. She went onto Hollywood, where she quickly became queen of the B Movies with a string of films including *Dance Girl, Dance* – the movie where she met her future husband, Cuban band leader Desi Arnaz, and they soon became the power couple of their day. Interestingly, she lost out the role of Scarlett O'Hara in *Gone With The Wind* (1939) to Vivien Leigh, which might have changed her career path dramatically.

By 1942 Ball was now sporting her famous red hair but her movie career had stagnated so Desi suggested she tried broadcasting. She got herself a role in a radio sitcom which was to become the template for *I Love Lucy* but the network wanted someone other than Desi to play her husband as they did not like the fact he was Hispanic; Lucille turned the job down flat.

Not to be downhearted, the couple worked on their own script and toured it around the country, test-running it in front of live audiences. CBS saw how strong *I Love Lucy* was and took them on, but Lucille and Desi had stipulations: to shoot in Hollywood not the current home of television, New York; to shoot on real film as opposed to the cheaper Kinescope, despite it resulting in both stars having to take a pay cut; and finally, that all the rights remained under their control at their new company, Desilu. Using film turned out to be a very clever decision as it did not degrade in the same way as Kinescope, ensuring the shows continued into syndication – repeats earning the couple millions of dollars over the years.

The wonderful Lucille Ball taught me women can be beautiful and silly all at the same time and that you can also be in charge of the business to boot.

MARIA BAMFORD (1970-)

By Bobbie Oliver

The Maria that can be described is not the Maria.

When you hear about a comic who is doing "something different" out there, they are almost always doing it within the existing framework of stand-up. When you watch Maria Bamford, you feel like she is doing something different on a whole new level, in a language that you never heard before. She is not writing jokes in words exactly, but in a mixed media that all comes from her amazing instrument: herself. She slips in and out of voices and characters and faces and moods. It's all in one long stream of consciousness – like memories in a mixed up mind that is so fragile, yet compelled to include you in that fragility.

My favourite comics are not afraid to be vulnerable on stage. Maria is not just vulnerable, she is naked and skinless. She shares every flaw, every insecurity, every heart breaking experience under a magnifying glass shoved in your face, and makes you feel what she feels whether you like it or not. She talks about feeling weird and inadequate when running into an old classmate (even at her level of success). On *Maria Bamford: The Special Special Special* she shares the tragic story about the accidental death of her beloved pug. She discusses relationships and loneliness in a raw, relatable hysterical way. She shares things that society tells us not to share. Maria is not just letting you witness her thought process; you are in her thought process. You *are* her thought process… like a weird scary magical dream you hope you never wake up from and that you could never begin to explain to anyone when you did. She seems to be exercising her demons and yours all at once. Yet you are so busy laughing, you don't even notice.

What lies underneath it all is a spot-on ability to write jokes that would kill even if they did not come from such a unique and layered delivery. Her art shows a real dedication to and a love of the craft of stand-up. She is a comic's comic. Maria also has one of the biggest hearts of anyone, especially in show business. Like most comics, she has anxieties and insecurities (which she openly discusses) that sometimes make dealing with people not her favourite thing. Yet she is the first person to reach a hand back to other comics and offer opportunities when she can. She is a genuine, honest, humble person and it shows in her craft.

Nothing I have written comes close to describing the art of Maria Bamford. An amazing influence on me and on hordes of other stand-ups – female and male – Maria Bamford is an experience, not an act.

ROSEANNE BARR (1952-)

"I did feminist comedy," states Roseanne Barr in Yael Koehn's book [19]. It's simply a point of fact. Roseanne explains that her decision to perform direct feminist comedy was a clear response to all the male comedy that she'd seen ever since she was a child. But she does admit that it took her several years to learn how to pitch feminist comedy in a way that audiences would respond well to.

She clearly hit the nail on the head, because she went on to be the first female stand-up from her era to write and appear in her own regular sitcom (*Roseanne*, 1988-1997), for which she won an Emmy and Golden Globe. *Roseanne* broke new ground in many ways, aside from having a woman at the helm behind the scenes. It focused on a working-class family who were struggling to make ends meet and lived in a ramshackle home, and the star of the show was a larger woman who didn't meet the entertainment industry's ideas of what a conventionally attractive woman would look like. As the character Roseanne Connor, Roseanne Barr played up to her self-given title of 'Domestic Goddess'.

For the first seven seasons of *Roseanne*, the show remained in the top ten of the TV ratings chart – so clearly Roseanne had tapped into what the public wanted and would accept, although she admits she had to fight hard to be able to make her own decisions about her show: "There's definitely damage to my nervous system from all that fighting [20]", adding: "They were trying to stop me from controlling my show [21]."

There's pretty much nothing that Roseanne can't turn her hand to. From writing and performing comedy, to producing and directing hit shows, and taking on cameos in other comedians' shows including *The Larry Sanders Show* (1993-1995) and *Portlandia* (2013). While in November 2014, Roseanne hosted Las Vegas' first ever all-female comedy solo show, *Lipschtick*, at the Venetian Resort.

SANDRA BERNHARD (1955-)

Emerging on the New York stand-up scene in the late 1970s where she was a regular at the Comedy Store, Sandra Bernhard became known for critiquing celebrity culture and mocking politicians. Her popularity led her to be a regular cast member on *The Richard Pryor Show* in 1977, which eventually catapulted her onto the coveted late night talk show sofas. However, Sandra's breakthrough moment was in 1983 when Martin Scorcese cast her as Robert De Niro's stalker in *The King of Comedy*.

Later in the 1980s, Sandra's live comedy shows became more performance art orientated and her influential solo show *Without You I'm Nothing* ran for six months off-Broadway in 1988, and inspired a film and album of the same name.

Described by the *New York Times* as "a living, breathing bonfire", in 1991 Sandra took a regular role in Roseanne Barr's sitcom *Roseanne* playing Nancy Bartlett until 1997. Nancy was the first ever openly gay character on a US sitcom.

CONNIE BOOTH (1944-)

Best known for her role as chambermaid Polly in the BBC's seminal 1970s' comedy series *Fawlty Towers*, a lot of people don't realise that Connie Booth also co-wrote the show.

American actor and writer Connie met her future husband John Cleese in 1968 while she was working as a waitress and he was over in New York trying to make it as a stand-up comedian. She went on to appear in several episodes of his cult comedy series *Monty Python* before they co-created the phenomenally successful and enduringly popular *Fawlty Towers*.

After the sitcom and their marriage ended in 1978, Connie turned to straight acting before training as a psychotherapist in 1995.

JO BRAND (1957-)

Having originally trained and worked as a psychiatric nurse, Jo Brand made the move to comedy in the mid-1980s saying: "I was aware of the dearth of women and wanted to get out there and do some material for the female audience [22]."

Her early stage name was 'The Sea Monster', but despite the unappealing moniker Jo became a popular face on London's alternative comedy circuit and started appearing on Channel 4's influential *Saturday Live* show.

With her trademark delivery of a bored and monotone voice, Jo referenced pop culture through her early sets. In more recent years, Jo has spoken out against the overwhelmingly male booking habits of many of the TV and radio panel shows, going so far as to flatly refuse to appear on shows such as the BBC's *Mock The Week*, where the few women who were on were edited out or talked over.

CARRIE BROWNSTEIN (1974-)
By Paul Duffus

As guitarist and singer in the band Sleater-Kinney, who formed in 1994 and continue to the present day, Carrie Brownstein is a respected and successful musician. In 2011 with *Portlandia*, the sketch show she created, writes and stars in alongside Fred Armisen, she also became one of the funniest people on television.

For context, Sleater-Kinney is not an average indie band and she is not an average guitarist. *Rolling Stone* called them the "best American punk band ever" and Carrie one of the "25 most underrated guitarists ever". This is not a failed *X Factor* contestant turning to musical theatre after crashing the pop career into the side of the mountain. This is a serious artist who expanded the range of her work in a quite unexpected way. In interviews Carrie has played down the unlikeliness of her shift from indie rock icon to brilliant comedian, but let's be clear how strange the move is. We're not going to be watching the Ian McKaye sitcom or Greg Ginn's sketch comedy hour anytime soon. What she has done is unique.

So she can rock, but is she funny? Well one of the thrills of Sleater-Kinney is the interplay between Carrie and Corin Tucker's guitars, the dynamics as they trade lines, contending and complementing one another, and it's very much the same between Carrie and Fred on *Portlandia*. At times he leads. As Candace of 'Candace and Toni', the feminist bookstore owners for whom no situation is simple or easy, Fred is a tangle of fury, always one non-incident away from burning the shop to the ground. It would be easy to be overshadowed but, as Toni, Carrie enhances his animation with a deadpan stillness and unanswerable indignation, whether it's chastising Aubrey Plaza for excessively penile hand gestures or accusing a confused Steve Buscemi of instigating a "back alley hooker/pimp transaction", ie buying something.

At other times Carrie goes full 'Eruption' while her partner plays rhythm. As Kath of 'Kath and Dave', the couple who pursue recreation with militaristic keenness, people who love nothing more than acute stress, Carrie is ferocious but never unsympathetic, undercutting Kath's psychotic enthusiasm with an endearing childishness. When she impatiently cajoles an outdoor cinema with cries of "COME ON, MOVIE! MAKE IT START!" in one of Kath's spontaneous bouts of singsong screaming, the performance is huge and crazy and somehow completely agreeable. Ultimately though the mania of Carrie's delivery creates the perfect space for Fred/Dave's understated, deadpan punchline, "You have a good singing voice," the pair matching and gilding each other's performances to a degree which completely belies their different levels of experience in sketch comedy.

KATHY BURKE (1964-)
By Marina O'Shea

Her eyes are small, spread out and sit at a relaxed half droop. Her hair rarely migrates from a short, messy crop, embodying the real just-rolled-out-of-bed look. Her lips are thin, and often pressed in a curl or her famous open-mouthed gape. She smokes like a train and swears like a geezer. Her gait is wide, bobbling along with a Whoopi Goldberg stance. Her ideal man is 'A plumber that can read'. As a person, she's everything you could describe as gritty, but with softness. She's Kathy Burke. And she's my hero.

In fact, she's more than a hero. She's an ordinary person. Making ordinary much loved by millions, she even makes it beautiful. Born in Islington in 1964, she has a blunt and striking charm with an honesty – on screen and in her writing – that draws people to her.

I, along with many other women I suspect, have a lot to thank her for. One of the defining moments of my life was playing a comic boy in a Theatre Festival so convincingly that the judging panel was lost for words when told I was, in fact, a little girl. It was 1992 – just before Kathy Burke came onto our screens as the teenage boy Perry on BBC1's *Harry Enfield and Chums*. The rest of my cast was blue-eyed, blonde curled dainty girls and striking young men. They regarded me as odd, alien, as I spoke my mind, had messy hair and chewed my sleeve while making jokes mostly to any chair or wall that was close by. But Kathy changed that: she is one of few comic actors – and a writer and director – who strive to find those female roles that have something more to them than stereotypical castings for women.

A walk through her golden moments for me, and I'm drawn to Waynetta the slob from sketch show *Harry Enfield and Chums* – the charisma of a flea and the social graces of the Pope on crack. Perry from the same series – the beautifully portrayed awkward teenage adolescent that makes you have to slap a small child to jolt you to remember she is in fact a woman. Her *Gimme Gimme Gimme* character, the loud-mouthed, dirty minded Linda La Hughes – reminding me of the Linda in me, flooring me with lines like: "I wouldn't mind him putting his hand up my skirt and moving my lips, if you know what I mean!" Then to the far end contrast: taking my breath away and making me feel every punch in the brutally honest role of a battered and defiant housewife in *Nil By Mouth*.

My respect for her as a comedy role model comes from her presence on screen which can not only hold its own weight against her male counterparts, but shines out above all others around her, male or female - whether in comedic parts or her aforementioned more serious award winning role in the 1997 British drama film *Nil by Mouth* (1997).

It fascinates me to watch Kathy in interviews, for no matter how big her fame grows, she remains a person with no fancy frills or airs. Her most beautiful quote? Easy: "What does love feel like? A joyful humiliation [23]."

She reminds me in her work that nothing else matters, not where you come from or how you got there – a person is a person – and that's it.

MARGARET CHO (1968-)
By Jess McCabe

Way back in the early 2000s, I picked up a secondhand book with a brash yellow and blue cover. It was called *I'm The One That I Want* and it was by Margaret Cho – at that time already a successful stand-up comic who had opened for Jerry Seinfeld and created and starred in a sitcom based on her family, which starred the first Asian American family on US television.

I didn't know about her success – or her just as public failures: the television studio that commissioned the sitcom quickly lost faith, taking the plot far from its origins in Margaret's stand up routines about her family and growing up. The studio wanted a wholesome story – Margaret's was not ("The closest I ever got to that was being a hole to some", she quips in the book.)

They also put Margaret under enormous pressure to lose weight, leading her to crash diet and eventual suffer kidney failure. And, one time in a memorable episode that made its way into her comedy routines, leading Margaret to adopt a permission-only diet that resulted in her shitting her pants in her car (this is so typically Margaret – making something so personal and awful into something hilarious). The show was a flop and led to a spiral of destruction that Margaret chronicles in her book, which culminated in being booed off stage after doing a stand-up routine at a university drunk.

Some of Margaret's work is just charming: talking about her upbringing in Castro, San Francisco, before she had heard that gay men existed yet, she writes: "I thought, 'that is so nice, they are fixing each other's zippers'." But a lot of other routines tap into darker moments. But lots of Margaret's jokes broke boundaries because, when so much of mainstream comedy (still!) thinks just saying something is racist is funny, she twists this around to laugh in the face of micro-aggressors, misogynists, body haters, racists, homophobes and other oppressors. One of her early famous sketches, Asian Chicken Salad, was about being on an aeroplane and watching the steward offer all the other passengers the option of Asian Chicken Salad. When they got to Margaret, the steward paused and said "chicken salad?" But it's funny.

I didn't know any of this yet when I picked up that book. But the title of that book, *I'm The One That I Want*, called out to me with its promise of winning self-acceptance the hard way. "I have been a longtime perpetrator of hate crimes against myself and I am turning myself in," she wrote. That was the start and the end. I couldn't get enough of Margaret. I bought her follow-up book. I read her website where she delighted in picking apart the sacks of hate mail she received, and talked about getting beautiful tattoos to stake a claim on her own body. I ordered the CD recordings of her shows. I booked tickets to her rare London performances as soon as they went on sale – and every show was packed out with an oh-so-appreciative audience.

Heroine worship is a difficult thing – we come to love our idols for what they've done, but it's almost an inevitability they will slip up sometimes. Margaret is no exception and she's been sent flying by so many problematic bananas over the last few years it's forced me to realign from total fangirl to a more realistic level of enthusiasm. It's not for me to forgive or excuse any of those moments, like the wince-inducing moment on American television when she 'joked' that "My eggs are jumping ship. They're like, 'Last one out is a retard'."' Later, she apologised: "I did a stellar job in disappointing countless others with my callous, witless tongue. I was thinking about myself solely, no one else, which I hate. I was way out of line."

When I first came across Margaret's work I did think she was perfect and wanted to love everything she said and did. Of course she's not perfect. Actually I was missing the point of Margaret. Her entire charm and appeal is based on that intense overwhelming honesty, including about her most painful moments.

BRIDGET CHRISTIE (1971-)

It's hard to pick a favourite Bridget Christie moment. But if I had to choose, it would be an unintentional highlight. The one when *The Daily Mail* accompanied a news story about King Charles II (you know, the long-dead 17th Century king) with a photograph of Bridget dressed as King Charles II while riding a horse (you know, those photographs that were invented in the 19th Century). The photo was from Bridget's poster for her 2008 Edinburgh show, *The Court Of King Charles II...* and quite clearly shows a woman in a costume hamming it up with a pen-drawn moustache. Perhaps this was the paper's revenge for Bridget's 2009 Edinburgh show *My Daily Mail Hell*, recounting her years spent working for the newspaper. More likely, it was stupidity. Either way, it was hilarious.

More recently, Bridget has unintentionally become the voice of feminism on the comedy circuit. Her award-winning, sold-out 2013 Edinburgh show *A Bic For Her* (performed in a No More Page 3 t-shirt) drew on such hot topics as the sexism of racing driver Stirling Moss, explaining to mock hecklers why FGM wasn't a suitable topic for a stand-up comedy show, and questioning how on earth the Brontë sisters managed to write anything decent when they didn't have an ergonomically designed pink pen with which to write. The follow-up 2014 show, *An Ungrateful Woman*, continued the theme while building on Bridget's fantastic platform to use humour to put feminist issues on the front pages

Bridget's subjects stemmed from her hit BBC Radio 4 show *Bridget Christie Minds The Gap*, where Fred MacAulay plays the role of the hapless mansplainer to perfection. Bridget's radio show has garnered not only a second series to date, but also a book deal. Watch this space.

RICHMAL CROMPTON (1890-1969)

Schoolteacher turned novelist Richmal Crompton is the woman behind the phenomenally enduring comic series of *Just William* books: a character who first appeared in print in 1919. William was a feisty and mischievous schoolboy who went on to star in 38 books by Richmal. The character was so popular that he was translated into nine languages and the books sold worldwide. They remain in print today.

As well as being one of the first women to graduate with a degree, Richmal was also a prominent suffragette. She never married, remained childfree and earned so much money from her writing that by the time she retired she was able to buy a country house for herself and her mother to live in. All the signs of a strong and independent woman.

MARION DAVIES (1897-1961)

Born in Brooklyn, New York City, Marion Douras adopted the surname Davies after spotting it on an estate agents' board believing that an English surname would stand her in better stead than her Greek birth name. Marion always wanted to be a star and began her career as a model before appearing in her first film in 1917: *Runaway Romany* for which she also wrote the script.

Marion tended to appear in light, comic films and rapidly won the hearts of her audiences, becoming a successful and bankable star by 1918. However, her romantic relationship with media tycoon William Randolph Hearst sometimes overshadowed her own career, although he formed Cosmopolitan Pictures (yes, Hearst is the publishing company that still owns *Cosmopolitan Magazine* to this day, that's not a coincidence) in order to further her filmmaking. While William wanted Marion to appear in costume dramas, she preferred to make comedies but to do so meant working for other companies.

Her role in the 1928 film *The Patsy* was an opportunity for Marion to showcase her hilarious imitations, which had previously been reserved for her friends. When her relationship with William soured in 1937, he responded by moving Cosmopolitan Pictures to another studio and away from Marion... who decided to take the opportunity to leave the film business and focus on charity work.

ELLEN DEGENERES (1958-)
By Kate Smurthwaite

Women are well equipped to be comedians: womanhood is quite an act. Waxing, starving yourself, uncomfortable footwear, painting on a whole new face, pretending we're interested in all the self-serving macho twaddle that so often passes for popular culture.

The problem for women isn't the skills then, it's the parts. The same old stereotypes: smiley girl next door, evil powerful temptress, ugly old hag (I can get through all of those in one afternoon!).

Stand-up comedy allows women to throw the stereotypes away. We write our own scripts and we always play the complicated lead. We play ourselves onstage, warts, genitals, genital warts and all. Not everyone can handle it.

Enough philosophy, now some herstory. In the 1980s in the deep south of the US, an incredible female performer arrived on the comedy scene. Her name was Ellen DeGeneres.

The 1980s may have been the least sexist decade since Boudicca abandoned her chariot and went back to knitting. Still no one knew what to do except to try and trim the charismatic personality into a sitcom character.

Ellen could play a quirky friend to some women who fitted the approved stereotypes a bit better. Provided with a non-threatening job running a bookstore, a neutral surname and a set of mix and match model-beautiful co-stars she was ready for consumption by the broader American, and global, public.

It shouldn't really have worked, it should have been Ellen with the edges knocked off, the best bits stripped away. But you can't keep a good woman down. And you shouldn't try to anyway. Using little more than a squeak of surprise or an unimpressed glance she won every laugh and built the comedy with her raw energy. Never cook energy. And she came across as so damn likable that the series was a huge hit.

Taking charge of the roles given to her both onscreen and off, Ellen came out as a lesbian in an era that was genuinely shocked by the news. The series was terminated and both she and Laura Dern, the straight actress who played her on-screen love interest, suddenly weren't getting work.

For many performers that would be the end of the story. But the warm, fun personality that had broken all the boring rules was exactly what the talk show circuit needed. A showcase for the real Ellen: deeply likable, bouncing with energy and still peppered with her quick-witted lines. It works so well you can't switch it off. It's magical and it's just Ellen, being herself.

GRACE DENT (1973-)

Journalist and author Grace Dent is quite possibly the funniest woman on Twitter (@gracedent), as her hilarious 2011 book *How To Leave Twitter* attested. She's the author of eleven books for teenagers including the *Diary Of A Snob* and *Diary of A Chav* series, and presenter of numerous TV and radio documentaries. But it's her TV columns for *The Guardian* and *The Independent* for which she is best loved.

Grace neither beats around the bush nor minces her words, as any restaurant that has suffered the ordeal of being reviewed by her for the *Evening Standard* (but failed to live up to her expectations) can confirm. Her ability to rip shreds off a ropey eaterie is second to none, and the delight for readers in consuming her words is unparalleled.

And we've got this far without even mentioning the unassuming yet sharp manner with which Grace conducts herself on the many TV and radio shows she appears, whether as an interviewee or as a pundit.

PHYLLIS DILLER (1917-2012)

Cutting her comedy teeth with spots on Californian radio and her 15-minute series *Phyllis Diller: The Friendly Homemaker*, future appearances alongside Bob Hope in the 1960s would help to secure Phyllis Diller the audiences she craved. While best loved for her stand-up comedy routines, Phyllis also starred in two TV sitcoms: *The Pruitts of Southampton* and *The Beautiful Phyllis Diller Show*.

Her career continued apace, with regular TV and film work – which, in 2000, won her the Lucy Award (named after Lucille Ball) at the Women in Film Awards, which was to celebrate her lifelong achievements in improving the perception of women on television.

By Rhodri Marsden

They say that women are funnier than men on Twitter. While I'm reluctant to make massive, sweeping generalisations of this kind (not least because that's the kind of thing that racists do) I'm inclined to agree. There seems to be a subtext to any tweets posted by men who profess to be funny – a sense that it's part of some over-arching strategy, that they're striving for their own television series, book deal or potential knighthood. While this is evidently not always the case, and while many women are equally driven by burning ambition, I find that women just seem to get on with being funny, almost accidentally funny, with a refreshing lack of narcissism that's both compelling and, weirdly, more funny.

Which brings me to @TheDollSays. Her Twitter account reveals nothing about who she is, or what she does. She tweets sporadically; at the time of writing she hasn't posted anything since 2012. She just meanders online, posts a few beautifully observed epithets that would make seasoned comedy professionals wonder why on earth they bother, and then she wanders off again, unconcerned by follower counts or whether she's engaging effectively with blue-ticked Twitterati.

This was the first tweet of hers that I saw. It was retweeted into my timeline, and shimmered with understated brilliance:

"Just said the words 'structural integrity' when describing a block of cheese. The wanker alarm sounded and my mum hit me with a mallet."

It's safe to say that at that moment I fell in love with her. Here are some more of her finest moments:

"If 'launching the royal barge' doesn't become a euphemism for taking a crap then this country is dead inside."

"Convince people you've run the London Marathon by spending this afternoon wrapped in tin foil then being insufferable at dinner parties."

"Just tried to fold a fitted sheet. I should have attempted something easier like doing long division on a trampoline while being shot at."

"A toddler on the bus today was having such a frighteningly huge tantrum, my ovaries handed in their notice and applied to be kidneys."

I met her once. I sent her a message suggesting a drink; she replied saying "Why not?" So we spent an evening getting mildly drunk in Clapham. Her name is Jo, she works in an office, she has no interest in becoming famous or earning money from her exceptional wit and doesn't really give a shit about Twitter either way. But she wins Twitter. She won it years ago. She's undisputed proof of the fact that the funniest people don't think they are. I think she's amazing.

DIANA DORS (1931-1984)

Wiltshire-born Diana Fluck was modeled in the buxom style of Marilyn Monroe, which secured her roles in sex comedy films… as well as what is euphemistically called glamour modeling.

Diana had enjoyed a promising start to her career when at the age of 14 she became the youngest ever person to be welcomed to the prestigious London Academy of Music and Dramatic Art, from where she graduated with impressive honours in the late 1940s. Once her career started to take off, she changed her surname to Dors: the name of her maternal grandmother. At the age of 16, Diana was signed to the Rank Organisation film studio and went on to appear in many of their films.

When appearing as a guest on Bob Monkhouse's BBC radio show *Calling All Forces*, Diana courted controversy by seemingly flirting outrageously with Bob and then letting slip a few double entendres during a live transmission. The BBC censors saw red and promptly issued a new policy of demanding that all future scripts be submitted for prior approval… and banning Diana from any future shows. However, what they failed to notice was the hysteria of the audience at Diana's behaviour and jokes… and ultimately she was allowed back on the Beeb. In 1951, the show was so successful that Bob and Diana toured it around German army bases.

By the mid-1950s, Diana's management played up to her buxom persona by repeatedly seeing her cast in sex comedies. And by the late 1950s she was based in Hollywood and working as an actor, until she discovered that a series of bad investments made on her behalf had left her hideously in debt. As a result, Diana returned to the UK and to the sex comedies that had made her so popular.

LENA DUNHAM (1986-)
By Danielle Ward

"In every generation there is a chosen one. She alone will stand against the vampires, the demons, and the forces of darkness. She is the Slayer." That's the opening narration from *Buffy The Vampire Slayer*, but I think it also fits the bill with Lena Dunham (sort of… swap the vampire stuff for misogyny). In a world that applauds Unilad, Robin Thicke and t-shirts sporting pro-rape slogans, Lena Dunham is the funny voice of a generation who'd rather not get felt up by a drunk on the subway, actually, thank you very much.

What makes Lena's work so brilliant is it's not a preoccupation with giving 20-something women a voice, it's an innate predisposition. She's not making a point, she just is being 28 in a world where this bullshit happens. That's not to say *Girls* is a rallying cry against injustice, it clearly isn't and it doesn't try to be, but by being so brutally, hysterically honest about what it's like to be a girl in her world, Lena also faces sexism head on. Plus the woman writes very funny sex scenes. Men write sexy sex scenes. Most of the sex I had in my 20s was not sexy. It was fist bitingly awful. And probably very funny to anyone watching (there *wasn't*. I made sure).

At lot has been made of how much Lena has achieved while being so young. She's not *Doogie Howser MD*! The Beatles were already starting to split up by the time they were her age. Uri Gagarin was 27 when he became the first man in space and no one goes on about him being precocious. Maybe if he'd been funny and a woman the haterz would have hated. Lena writes funny, honest dialogue and shows the difficult post-university years in all their horrific glory. She has not been into space. Yet.

JENNY ÉCLAIR (1960-)

In 2013, comedian and writer Jenny Eclair ruffled a few feathers when she decided to ring in to BBC Radio 4's *Woman's Hour* having become incensed after listening to the show at home. What had got under her skin was the way former *Have I Got News For You* producer Jo Bunting was defending the show's scarcity of female panelists by saying the women they asked often didn't want to take part. Having already taken to Twitter to vent steam, Jenny picked up the phone and spoke direct to Jo live on air. Jenny's response to Jo's claim that women didn't ever want to take part in the satirical news quiz was: "Well, you've never asked me!" Despite being a hugely popular comedian since 1983, by 2013 Jenny was still waiting for her first invitation to *Have I Got News For You* (which launched in 1990 so had been on air for 23 years by this time).

Although it takes a little while for the effects to trickle through, it was noticeable that early the following year, in 2014, BBC executive Danny Cohen announced that all BBC TV and radio panels would have at least one woman on the show. Around the same time, BBC Radio 4's *Today* show had had the audacity to tackle a whole series of subjects relating to women (eg breast cancer in women, provision of contraception to teenage girls) without once thinking to invite a woman on to discuss these topics. So it doesn't seem like a huge leap of faith to add Jenny's phone call to Jo Bunting into the mix of things that caused Danny Cohen to make his infamous announcement.

Jenny is, of course, more than a mere catalyst for change. She is first and foremost a comedian, having started her stage career at university by performing punk poems. This quickly led to a career in stand-up comedy, and in 1995 she was the first woman to win the coveted Perrier Award at the Edinburgh Fringe Festival (in 2013, Bridget Christie became the third woman to win the prize... with Laura Solon being the second woman in 2005). Thanks to her roles in the phenomenally popular TV and stage show *Grumpy Old Women*, Jenny has become the face of joyous complaint – and we love her for it.

NORA EPHRON (1941-2012)

In the 1960s and 1970s, the women's movement generated a huge volume of discussion and writing that ultimately inspired much of the feminist humour that we now have. Central to this was American writer Nora Ephron, whose 1975 collection of essays *Crazy Salad* is a hilarious and staunchly pro-woman book that remains popular today.

Her loosely autobiographical 1983 novel *Heartburn* topped the bestseller lists, but still won her criticism for being a "thinly disguised novel" about the breakdown of her real-life second marriage. Yet as Nora wrote in the foreword to the 2004 edition: "I've noticed over the years that the words 'thinly disguised' are applied mostly to books written by women. Let's face it, Philip Roth and John Updike picked away at the carcasses of their early marriages in book after book, but to the best of my knowledge they were never hit with the thinly disguised thing [24]." Just another example of how behaviour that is acceptable for men is completely unacceptable for women.

The feminist movement on both sides of the Atlantic has increased our awareness of everyday sexism in all its many forms. But more recently, comedians are using humour to draw attention to the stifling sexism they endure on a daily basis. Caitlin Moran, Bridget Christie, Nadia Kamil are just the first three names to spring to mind, but there are hundreds more. But back in the 1970s, Nora was writing cuttingly fantastic essays such as 'Dealing With The, Uh, Problem' where she ridiculed the advertising industry for its bizarre and patronising way of marketing tampons and sanitary towels to women – as if periods were a problem that the men at the factory had now solved for the willing ladies. Nora had an amazing talent for making feminism funny, despite the age-old myth that feminists are sour-faced harridans.

As a scriptwriter, Nora was nominated for three Academy Awards and was the voice behind box office smashes including the Meg Ryan trilogy *When Harry Met Sally* (1989), *You've Got Mail* (1998) and *Sleepless In Seattle* (1993). Nora's skill was in taking the ordinary, everyday things that affected women and turning them into overblown absurdities that prompted the audience to laugh at themselves as much as with the characters.

In addition to excelling as a female scriptwriter in Hollywood, Nora also achieved the rare feat for a woman in the film industry by being a producer and director as well.

TINA FEY (1970-)

By Paul Duffus

Artistic achievement cannot be measured by awards because they are often at least in part determined by non-artistic considerations, for example, industry politics, commercial influences and so on. So here's a list of some of the awards Tina Fey has won over the past two decades: eight Emmys, two Golden Globes, five Screen Actors Guild Awards, and four Writers Guild of America Awards. She's also the youngest recipient of the Mark Twain Prize for American Humour, previous winners of which include Steve Martin, Lily Tomlin and Richard Pryor.

Either she exerts a Kim Jong-Il-esque influence over the entertainment industry whereby heads roll if worship of those famous spectacles is not regular and lavish, or more likely Tina Fey is not just supremely funny but also one of the most significant comedy talents of her generation. She is certainly the most acclaimed.

It is as the creator, head writer and star of *30 Rock* that Tina is best known. The sitcom ran for seven seasons and although it never achieved the all-conquering ratings of a *Seinfeld*, its cultural impact and its influence in defining the style and tone of a particular time in television comedy was just as great. Like *Seinfeld*, it was the show of its era that critics and discerning comedy fans could agree upon, of which Tina's overflowing trophy cabinet is evidence.

30 Rock was intelligent, articulate and culturally literate, as likely to launch into an acute satire of the left and right wing mores affecting the US at the time as to cook up a surreal storyline involving Jane Krakowski dating a drag version of herself. The sharpness of the writing reflected Tina's previous work as the anchor of *Saturday Night Live*'s *Weekend Update* segment, a cultural touchstone of drollness and intelligence long before *The Daily Show*. In 1999 she became *Saturday Night Live*'s first female head writer.

Another joy of *30 Rock* was the dexterity and apparent ease of Tina's performances, talent honed through years of work with Second City, Chicago's famous improvisational comedy troupe. Even while surrounded by experts like the aforementioned Jane Krakowski, and other *30 Rockers* such as Tracy Morgan and Alec Baldwin, Tina shone. Her perfect timing, her clowning, all go without saying, but you need someone to bust out a casual Joni Mitchell impression? Or be a spaced out Princess Leia obsessive? Maybe do some Walken? Whatever the scenario, Tina showed unmatched versatility and skill.

The unparalleled writing CV, which includes movies and a best selling memoir, would in itself mark Tina Fey out as a brilliant talent. Throw in her virtuoso performances on *30 Rock* and you have a peerless comedian, someone who appears to be the best at whatever she chooses to do. Even Sarah Palin might have to agree with that.

HELEN FIELDING (1958-)

Have you read the *Bridget Jones* books? You must have. Or at least seen the films with Renée Zellweger in the title role.

Journalist, novelist and screenwriter Helen Fielding created *Bridget Jones* as a character for a column in *The Independent* newspaper in 1995. The three *Bridget Jones* books have gone on to be published in 40 countries and sold more than 15 million copies. And the original book has been named as one of the ten defining books of the 20th Century by the *Guardian*, which is quite some claim to make – especially when the others on that list include John Steinbeck, George Orwell and Anne Frank [25].

Helen started out as a researcher and producer for the charity Comic Relief, which is where she met Richard Curtis who went on to pick up the *Bridget Jones* books and turn them into blockbuster films. Helen's debut novel *Cause Celeb* (1994) was inspired by her time in Eastern Sudan, and although not a huge hit at the time of publication the book showcased Helen's capacity as a comic writer.

After creating the character of Bridget for *The Independent* in 1995 (who had asked Helen to write a column about her own single life in London... an idea Helen immediately rejected), the columns proved so popular that Helen was quickly asked to write the debut diary, and when the paperback came out in 1997 it was a word-of-mouth soar-away success. I remember reading it shortly after it came out, after being recommended it by a colleague in the bookshop I was then working in, and spending my day off holed up in my bedroom, unable to tear myself away from the laugh-out-loud pages. If you need confirmation of the comedy value of Bridget and Helen, just read the blue soup story in the first diary. You can thank me later.

There was comic value in everything that Bridget did. From the angry sneers that she stabbed into her diary about the smug Mark Darcy to the helpless way she fell down the fireman's pole on live TV… Bridget's can-do attitude is what makes her such a star. But she'd have been nothing without Helen. Obviously.

The Edge Of Reason followed in 1999 and *Mad About The Boy* in 2013. Both were also populated with comedy gold… although by the time we reached *Mad About The Boy* and (spoiler alert) Bridget is a 50-something widow struggling to bring up two young children alone, the book is also filled with some real tear-jerking moments.

The reason Bridget was so popular a character was because she spoke to her readers. As Helen said in *The Guardian* in 2013, looking back: "It's more wonderful still if Bridget has done something to counteract the culture of perfection and make people feel it's alright just to be alright [26]."

Some have said she was a product of her time and that Helen should have left Bridget in the 1990s… but the fact *Mad About The Boy* topped the bestsellers lists in 2013 suggests otherwise.

DAWN FRENCH & JENNIFER SAUNDERS (1957- & 1958-)

Lifelong comedy partners Dawn French and Jennifer Saunders met at college in 1977 and, after working their way around the alternative comedy circuit of London with a bizarre combination of acts, in 1987 the duo won their own BBC sketch series, uncomplicatedly called *French and Saunders*. This was five years after their first appearance in Channel 4's spoof comedy drama series *The Comic Strip Presents…* (which premiered on the very first night of the new TV station), and their roles in the short-lived sitcom *Girls On Top*, which Dawn and Jennifer co-wrote with long-time future collaborator Ruby Wax.

But it was through their eponymously titled sketch show that Dawn and Jennifer reached a really huge audience. And despite an admittedly ramshackle first series, by the second running they had found their feet and established the set pieces that would become series regulars for the next 20 years. Dawn was the overly jolly one; Jennifer the aloof and cynical one. And nowhere was this more apparent than in the living room set, The White Room, where Jennifer tended to recline on a couch in her blue toweling turban, only for Dawn to burst into the room and bring some new level of chaos to Jennifer's lazy life. It might not sound much written down but it was always comedy gold.

French and Saunders holds a deep affection for me for many reasons. After *The Young Ones* (in which Dawn and Jennifer were guests), it was the first comedy show that I remember videoing and watching again and again each morning while shoveling in my cereal before school. Most of the adult jokes passed me by at that age, but I was captivated by these two funny women on the telly. A handful of friends at school felt the same and we would quote the sketches at length to each other in classrooms, even though a lot of the jokes were far from suitable for our young ears. That didn't matter – there was something about this comedy duo that spoke to us. And as we got older, we realised what it was.

What it was that stood out to us about Dawn and Jennifer was their seemingly casual sense of indifference to the world around them. They sent up the pop stars that we also loved to hate (Bros! Sonia! Madonna!). They were sending up sexism, classism, the rich, the cruel… And they did it in a blunt, no-nonsense style. But they also gently mocked those they admired (Jane Asher, Thora Hird, June Whitfeld and co), who often appeared in cameo roles on the show, pretending to explode with rage at the unthinking duo.

After decades of watching *French And Saunders* on telly, on video and on DVD, it was a delight to see their final live stage show, *Still Alive!*, at the Theatre Royal Drury Lane, London, in 2008. My friend Abbie and I went together: our shared passion for Dawn and Jennifer was one of the things that cemented our friendship when we met at school in Somerset back in 1991, and our nicknames for each other to this day are still Janet P and Tanya – after the duo's 'She Rappers' sketch from 1990, where they play truly appalling Cookie Crew-style rappers who leave guest star DJ Mark Moore completely lost for words at how shit they are.

It's impossible to mention French and Saunders without also expressing adoration for their pitch perfect piss takes of the biggest films of the time. Jennifer's take on Jodie Foster in *Silence Of The Lambs* is rivaled only by Dawn's stuttering Hannibal Lecter. But to my mind the finest spoof they created was the genius *The House Of Idiot* recreation of the BBC's then-popular Sunday-night fashion drama *The House Of Elliot*. Even now, neither my mum nor I can walk down a flight of steps in front of each other without pretending to stoop and giggle. Even now, neither Abbie nor I can mention the word 'buttons' without feeling the need to add, "You can't feed children buttons, Tilly!" And if I ever meet someone called Jack, I have to call wistfully into thin air, "Jack!" – and my new friend wonders what's wrong with me.

After the sketch show started to wane, Dawn and Jennifer tried separate projects. Jennifer had a huge international hit on her hands thanks to *Absolutely Fabulous*, spawned from a short *French And Saunders* sketch. While Dawn found success as *The Vicar of Dibley*. Neither has strayed far from the public's heart and both have bestselling memoirs to their names.

Although French and Saunders are obvious favourites to pick for this book, they're genuinely my most favourite female comedians of all time, ever. They inspired a love of comedy in me at a time when I was too young to notice whether the performer was male or female, instead I simply knew I loved who these people were. And I've continued to love their comedy – whether it's re-watches of old shows or their new work – to this day. And you can't put a price on 30+ years of laughter.

JANEANE GAROFALO (1964-)

Janeane Garofalo, with her red lipstick and biker boots, spearheaded a new age of Generation X stand-ups in the 1990s. With disregard for the until-then traditional style of male comedians, Janeane worked hard to take her style of stand-up out of the male-dominated clubs and instead move it into coffee shops, bookshops and anywhere where the comics could regain control of the performance. In this way, Janeane was able to deliver a storytelling style of comedy rather than a set-up and joke style of comedy, which was what the clubs wanted and the men delivered.

But for Janeane, the big breaks did not come through stand-up but when Ben Stiller cast her in his self-titled sketch show (1992-1993), and then Garry Shandling cast her as a series regular on *The Larry Sanders Show* (1992-1997) – both of which highlighted her talent as a comedy actor. This was an exciting time for women generally, with the Grunge music scene from Seattle giving a platform for female-fronted bands such as Hole, The Breeders and Throwing Muses, and the ensuing Riot Grrrl scene.

STELLA GIBBONS (1902-1989)

Author, journalist and poet Stella Gibbons is best known for her bestselling comic novel *Cold Comfort Farm* (1932), which invites comparisons to Jane Austen's work for Stella's use of controlled wit.

Cold Comfort Farm was born out of Stella's time as a book reviewer for *The Lady* magazine, at which she became known as a rather caustic reviewer who was critical of the fashion for novels romanticising idyllic country childhoods. So she set about writing a parody of the genre, resulting in *Cold Comfort Farm*. The book became an instant critical hit and a bestseller, with at least one reviewer presuming that the book must have been written by a man because it was too clever for a woman to have written it – the assumption was that 'Stella Gibbons' was the pen name for Evelyn Waugh.

However, Stella thought of herself as more of a serious poet than a comic novelist, and also published several collections of poetry. Although she did go on to write several more satirical novels, including *Tricky* (1942), before writing two follow-ups to the *Cold Comfort* series: *Christmas at Cold Comfort Farm* (1940) and *Conference at Cold Comfort Farm* (1949).

WHOOPI GOLDBERG (1955-)
By Gabriela Staniszewska

Born Caryn Johnson in 1955, the woman who became Whoopi Goldberg is not only a comedian but also an ardent political activist. Coming to the fore in the 1980s, when African-American comedians were taking to the stage following the phenomenal success of Richard Pryor, racial activism has always been central to Whoopi's stand-up routines.

Her shows often utilise her acting skills, and consistently riff on being a social outcast. Her remarkable 1985 show *Back To Broadway* was way ahead of its time, from the issues surrounding single motherhood and abortion, to the worries of a young African-American girl who wonders why she can't have long blonde hair like the women on TV. Whoopi's stand-up sets are always three things: hilarious, sad and powerful. In her own words: "Sometimes you have to be an entertaining activist to get attention."

Whoopi first stepped onto the worldwide stage in 1985 playing Celie Johnson in the film *The Colour Purple*. Then she went on to star in *Jumping Jack Flash* (1986), *Ghost* (1990) and *Sister Act* (1992). In all these movies, Whoopi plays a misfit who triumphs over adversity and refuses to conform to the rules. An African-American woman who falls in love with a white British spy; an oppressed, early 20th Century wife in the Deep South; a con-woman who turns out to be genuine; and a nightclub singer trying to hide among nuns. Again... hilarious, sad and powerful.

One of my favourite stories about Whoopi is her reason for taking the role of Guinan in *Star Trek: Nemesis* (2002). As a young girl, Whoopi says she saw Lt Uhura on TV and shouted to her mother: "Momma! There's a black lady on TV and she ain't no maid!" When the role came up, Whoopi specifically asked to audition, citing that "without *Star Trek*, people would think there were no black people in the future".

Maybe being a seminal African-American comedian in the 1980s, loudly and hilariously making your socio-political point with a quick wit and a smattering of well chosen swear words overshadowed Whoopi's gender? In her case, which is more impertinent to the surrounding patriarchal society: that she is black or that she is a woman? She would likely say both. Asked in an interview how she stays true to herself, Whoopi thinks for a second before responding: "What choice do I have?"

She has pioneered her own niche, taken the reins as an outcast and driven her life where she wanted it to go, not where society wanted her to fit. That she is now one of America's most prominent talk show hosts is no small feat. Never afraid to say the right thing, Whoopi is a legend in both comedy and self-affirmation.

JOYCE GRENFELL (1910-1979)

A wartime entertainer, Joyce Grenfell and her pianist toured the world performing their comedy songs for British troops stationed abroad. She was so popular with the troops that after the war Joyce was offered a number of film roles, which she took up alongside her flourishing career as a musical comedian.

Joyce also worked as a comedy writer for the BBC before making some satirical *Listen With Mother*-esque sketches, working on TV alongside comedy stars such as Alistair Sim and Margaret Rutherford and then appearing in the *St Trinians* film franchise (1954-1960).

But what Joyce is best remembered for are her witty monologues and one-woman shows. While initially seeming to be light and silly, Joyce's comedy often carried a more serious message about topics such as how society demeans women and their work.

CICELY HAMILTON (1872-1952)

By Naomi Paxton

"No doubt there are women in this room who have felt like myself, that the attraction of men was not the only thing that would bring us happiness in this world. For me that day was the beginning of my life..." (*The Vote*, 15 April 1911).

I first encountered the wonderful Cicely Hamilton while researching the role of professional theatre in the Votes for Women movement. Her most well known suffrage play *How The Vote Was Won*, written in 1909 in collaboration with fellow suffragist Christopher St John, imagines a general strike of women across the UK, has great parts for women and is funny, fast paced and clever. Her other comic plays such as *Pot and Kettle* (1909) and *Jack and Jill and a Friend* (1911) shrewdly charm and entertain the audience while opening their eyes to the absurdities of the inequalities of women's lives. Her writing often makes me laugh out loud – she has a keen eye for caricature, social tropes and class structures as well as a dry wit that makes her work both accessible and challenging. She also writes with empathy and warmth – her characters are never without charm and her fierce intellect cuts through sentimentality.

Cicely was a member of the Women's Freedom League, a founder member of both the Women Writers Suffrage League and the Women's Tax Resistance League and an Executive Committee member of the Actresses' Franchise League. She defined herself as a feminist rather than a suffragist and was always more interested in the broader campaign for economic and social equality for women. Her book *Marriage As A Trade* (1909) is a passionately argued and stylish polemic about male/female relationships that still feels relevant today.

As with all her work, her thoughtfulness, honesty and integrity shines through. Cicely's experiences on tour as a young actress opened her eyes to the realities and struggles of working class women and the limited opportunities for women of all backgrounds. Never afraid to respond to or reflect upon controversial issues, she published six novels, 17 non-fiction books and wrote over 15 plays. During WW1 Cicely helped to found the Scottish Women's Hospital in France, nursed soldiers at the Somme and was part of the Women's Auxiliary Army Corps. After the war she worked as a freelance journalist, published several European travelogues and wrote for the feminist journal *Time and Tide*, using her writing as a platform to campaign for birth control for women and the legalisation of abortion.

Talented, bold, compassionate, versatile, insightful and with a flair for using humour to create a common ground for communication – Cicely Hamilton's life and work is a constant inspiration and challenge to me as a feminist and as a performer.

MIRANDA HART (1972-)

Although her comedy style inspires strong opinions in many, it is impossible to deny that Miranda Hart is one woman who has made huge inroads into the British comedy psyche. Her phenomenally popular sitcom *Miranda* (2009-2015) ran for three series, with a few seasonal specials, and won ever-increasing audiences. The visual comedy pairing of tall and gangly Miranda with her diminutive sidekick Stevie (Sarah Hadland) was at the heart of the show, along with Miranda's on-off relationship with dishy chef Gary (Tom Ellis).

What made *Miranda* so successful was how it drew on the influences of comedy past – such as with Miranda's slapstick comedy style, clowning and plentiful physical gags, as well as the fact she quite literally ran a joke shop. The closing credits always rolled above a 'You have been watching' title card, reminiscent of 1970s and 1980s sitcoms such as *Hi-De-Hi* and *Dad's Army*, before flashing across the different cast members' faces. And nostalgia is never out of fashion. Just ask Peter Kay.

Hot on the heels of her TV success, Miranda sold out an arena tour in 2012 – a move that seemed unprecedented for such a relatively new name on the comedy circuit, and for one who hadn't seemingly done the tried and tested trudge around endless festivals and small halls. But Miranda pulled it off and stormed into London's sold-out O2 Arena.

HATTIE HAYRIDGE (1959-)

Although best known for playing Hilly in the TV sitcom *Red Dwarf* (1989-1992), Hattie Hayridge started out as – and remains – a hardworking and highly sought after stand-up comedian. She came through on the UK circuit in the late 1980s alongside other rising stars such as Jo Brand and Linda Smith, and continues to work endlessly.

Hattie wandered into London's Comedy Store one night in 1985 where she was bitten by the comedy bug and ended up signing up for a series of workshops there – alongside Paul Merton, Mike Myers and Julian Clary. It was 1986 before Hattie wrote her first few minutes of stand-up material, inspired by a cheating ex-boyfriend, which she performed on the spot at an open mic night in Highgate. A week later she performed her second gig at the Comedy Store – for which she had so little confidence that she didn't even bother to take her coat off.

Before long, Ben Elton was helping her hone her set and Hattie went on to appear on *Friday Night Live* (1988) – a Channel 4 show that provided a first TV platform for a host of soon-to-be respected alternative comedians such as Emo Phillips and Chris Barrie (who would become Rimmer in *Red Dwarf*).

JESSICA HYNES (1972-)

By Tiernan Douieb

People say you should never meet your heroes, as a warning that they may not live up to quite how you imagine them to be. A couple of years ago I was lucky enough to be doing warm-up work on a children's TV show that Jessica Hynes was a guest on.

I had to shout at the audience and get them cheering before Jessica joined the main cast onstage. The kids were seated quite far away from the stage and keeping them interested required rather a lot of work. Except when Jessica was on. Her natural energy brought a life to the show that caused the kids to focus. Not only did she shine during filming but in between takes she was friendly, chatty and often very naturally funny.

After the show Jessica raced to get the main acts' autographs for her kids and I sheepishly went to ask her for a picture. She happily obliged and I quickly realised you shouldn't meet your heroes, mainly because if you do you tend to gibber on about being a fan and generally make no sense whatsoever.

Jessica is, as far as I'm concerned, one of the finest comedy actors and writers that we've had in the UK over the last 15 years. *Spaced* was, and still is, one of the most relevant, clever and hilarious sitcoms aimed at the 20- and 30-somethings of my generation. Jessica Hynes' and Simon Pegg's writing managed to be poignant without being cheesy; surreal and imaginative while still being grounded and honest.

Most importantly, Daisy was a wonderful sitcom character who stood her own ground, was funny for her own reasons and a well-rounded real person when so many lesser sitcoms would've charged down the 'she's the token girl in a boy's house' boring easy route. And she played *Tekken*. I've always wondered how autobiographical Daisy was, as Jessica played her with such aplomb, wringing so many laughs from simple facial expressions or physical foibles.

Jessica is a constant mark of quality in whatever she's in, from her endlessly enthusiastic Siobhan in *Twenty Twelve* to her role in *Doctor Who* as Joan Redfern. I still don't think the series has recovered from her refusing to go on David Tenant's travels with him. Then there's *Son Of Rambow*, *Up The Women* and the wonderfully dark *Lizzie and Sarah*. I'm still aiming to find which executive refused to commission that and send them horrible things.

I would kill for the ability as a comedian to warm and tickle an audience half as much as Jessica does with a look or a tone of voice. *Spaced* changed how I saw comedy and I'm forever grateful for it. That's what I would have liked to have said to Jessica Hynes, as my grin at meeting her enveloped my face. But instead I blurbed: "I think you're brilliant" many times and then ran away to hide somewhere in shame. Never ever meet your heroes

HATTIE JACQUES (1922-1980)
By Estella Tincknell

Born in 1922, Hattie Jacques was a gifted comedian and actor who is now largely remembered for her roles as an overweight, strict and often lovelorn battleaxe in the British *Carry On* series of low-budget comedy films made between 1958 and 1973. Hattie's success began in radio, first as Sophie Tuckshop in *It's That Man Again* (1939-49) and later as the domestically inept Griselda Pugh in *Hancock's Half Hour* (1954-8), a character whose Sunday lunch was a source of existential despair for the fictional Hancock household. Hattie was thus already typecast by the time she appeared as the domineering Captain Clark in *Carry On Sergeant*, the first of the eponymous series, in 1958. Yet her star persona was more complex than might initially appear.

Indeed, Hattie was a glamorous and attractive woman with an ability to switch her voice from cut-glass clarity to breathy suggestiveness in an instant. A quality of underlying sweetness also made her immensely likeable. This meant that her position within the *Carry On* films mobilised profound contradictions around gender and power: on the one hand, her roles frequently positioned her as a stereotypically sexually frustrated authority figure; on the other, they offered the pleasurably transgressive spectacle of her as an unconventional, sympathetic and clearly desiring woman.

Her role as Matron in *Carry On Nurse* (1959), *Carry On Doctor* (1967) and *Carry On Matron* (1972) has become defining, both for Hattie herself and for the hospital matron as cultural icon, a figure whose disappearance has since been cast as a symptom of the decline of the NHS.

Indeed, it is Hattie's embodiment of starch-capped certitude that continues to be affectionately invoked as the symbol of a well-run hospital. Yet Matron is also the would-be seductress of Kenneth Williams's horrified Dr Tinkle. In a memorable scene in *Doctor*, the large-bosomed Hattie, clad in a black negligee, entices Tinkle into her bedroom and forces the reluctant medic onto her bed with the immortal lines: "I want to give you my all" to which he (inevitably) replies "I don't want your all, I don't even want a little bit of you." While this scene is within a timeworn tradition and seems initially to invite a collective shudder at middle-aged female desire, because Hattie invests the role of Matron with genuine romantic longing and dignity it is also imbued with the poignant recognition that for many 'matrons' romantic love was sacrificed to professional commitment.

This ability to turn stereotypical, potentially anti-feminist figures into proto-feminist heroines reappears in Hattie's own favourite of the series, *Carry On, Cabby* (1963), wherein her character Peggy Hawkins sets up a rival all-female taxi company, Glamcabs, in order to force her workaholic cabdriver husband (Sid James) to take notice of her – and proves that she can beat him at his own game while she is about it.

Hattie's latter years were focused on TV comedy, most importantly in the suburban surrealist sitcom *Sykes* (1972-9), in which she played Eric Sykes's naively cheerful twin sister. The programme showcased her comic talent and secured 17 million viewers at its peak. Sadly, it was ended by Hattie's premature death in 1980, aged 58. Hattie lives on through the continuing popularity of the *Carry On* films, however, and it is as Matron that she has been immortalised.

ALLISON JANNEY (1959-)
By Timon Singh

I have always been attracted to women who are able to creatively insult me. I'm sure there are legion of psychiatrists that would be able to link this to some unresolved childhood issue relating to my mother, but it has also translated into a love for a certain type of actors.

To me there is nothing funnier (or sexier) than a woman who can deliver a witty put down. Whether it's Bette Davis declaring that "peace and quiet is for libraries" in *All About Eve*, Christina Applegate going toe-to-toe with Will Ferrell in the creative insult department in *Anchorman: The Legend of Ron Burgundy* or Emma Stone calling a bitchy school colleague an "abominable twat" in *Easy A*, nothing is more likely to have me howling in laughter than a sarcastic one liner.

It is for that reason that, for me, the funniest actor to ever grace the screen is Allison Janney.

Best known as the towering press secretary CJ Cregg in the best TV show ever made *The West Wing*, Allison is blessed with the double whammy of comedy: the ability to do a great pratfall and to deliver an insult that cuts its victim to the quick.

In one of my favourite scenes in the series, CJ confronts Josh Lyman, Deputy Chief of Staff to the President of the United States of America, when he finds out he has stupidly been posting on a public online forum. Not only does she verbally chastise him, but she compares him to Jack Nicholson in *One Flew Over A Cuckoo's Nest* in that he may have had a pre-frontal lobotomy and she may now have to smother him with a pillow. Film reference and a devastating insult! Double win.

Allison really has it all. She can do any kind of funny, which I think is the key to being a comedy genius. She can do witty, oddball, physical comedy and, if necessary, emotional depth. Plus she plays Emma Stone's mother in *The Help*, and if that's not a perfect representation of her impact on the next generation of female comics I don't know what is.

MARIAN KEYES (1963-)

One of the most successful female novelists alive, Irish author Marian Keyes is often misbranded as nothing more than a chick-lit writer. However, her books cut much deeper than that. Themes of domestic violence and alcoholism run through some of her novels, alongside the recurring central thread of a young woman overcoming a variety of obstacles on her way to romantic triumph. Yes, that does sound like a chick-lit novel. But it is Marian's gentle turn of phrase, and sensitive wit that makes her capable of handling grim and serious topics in an accessible and readable way – meaning these often unpleasant topics, which are regularly swept under the carpet on account of not being very sexy, reach a wider audience.

Marian has since said that she finds it easier to be a funny writer than to be anything else and she thinks her funny bones are genetic. She says in *The Guardian* that she inherited a way of constructing sentences from her mother that just *is* funny: "I think, also, coming from Ireland – it's a huge cliche but I think we have a different vocabulary and we structure our sentences according to the rhythms of the old language we used to speak. It's more colourful and more entertaining [27]."

JANE KRAKOWSKI (1968-)
By Paul Duffus

Jane Krakowski is a comedy-Terminator. As Jenna Maroney in *30 Rock*, no matter how prolix the dialogue, how idiotic the scenario, or how ridiculous the song, she kills with a degree of efficiency that sets her apart from her not inconsiderably talented co-stars. She just makes it all – the vocal acrobatics, the jumps in tone, the tongue twister jokes – seem so simple.

Her performances on the show exhibit an ease borne from years of work and training. As with Tracy Morgan and Tracy Jordan, in many ways Jenna is an hysterically exaggerated version of Jane. While Jenna is a grown-up stage school brat who apparently attended the Royal Tampa Academy of Dramatic Tricks and spent her childhood fighting her way through pageants and talent contests at the whip of her dysfunctional mother, Jane is a trained actor, singer, and dancer who attended the somewhat more legitimate Professional Children's School, which was founded to serve New York's young actors, and the Mason Gross School of Arts at Rutgers.

Tracy may have been the *30 Rock* character obsessed with EGOTing (the phenomenon of winning an Emmy, a Grammy, a Tony and an Oscar) but her versatile talent is such that Jane is the member of the *30 Rock* cast most likely to do it in real life. In 2003 she won her first Tony for the role of Carla in the Broadway revival of *Nine*. The point is that Jenna is a parody of a Broadway hoofer, but if the actor playing the role was not in fact a world class singer-dancer-actor herself, then the joke wouldn't work.

Who else could have sang out the very final episode of *30 Rock* as Jane did? The material, *The Rural Juror* song, was an intentional mess of incomprehensible nonsense lyrics with a joyous chorus and a strangely touching coda. It was funny, but it was also designed to serve the serious purpose of setting the emotional tone for the show's closing scenes. With that heavy responsibility at stake, you've got to call in a professional, and Jane sang *The Rural Juror* song as if it were the last night of a winning run at the Gershwin, emoting the garbled lines with a force that would put Anne Hathaway in the shade. The finales of beloved TV shows usually go off like wet firecrackers, but somehow Jane singlehandedly gave *30 Rock* the dramatic, beautiful and hilarious ending it deserved.

MARIE LLOYD (1870-1922)
By Louise Wingrove

In his 1922 London Letter 'Marie Lloyd', TS Eliot explains: "…no other comedian succeeded so well in giving expression to the life of that audience (…) It was, I think, this capacity for expressing the soul of the people that made Marie Lloyd unique and that made her audiences, even when they joined in the chorus, not so much hilarious as happy."

What set Marie Lloyd apart from other acts was the same attribute that made her 'Our Marie' – her understanding of her audience. Like many music hall performers she was an East Ender, born in Hoxton. She knew the problems faced by her audience and how to show them that she understood. Often noted for her beauty, crude humour and flirty performances, Marie is most discussed for her sauciness. There is no doubt that her alluring costumes and playful personality made this true.

Yet, unlike many other music hall artists, her act was not based on exaggeration or the grotesque. She used very specific movements and tones of voice to get the most out of her songs and show her innate understanding for how the people lived. This allowed her to include subtle details about things such as the contents of a charwoman's handbag or, during her song *The Tale Of The Skirt*, ways to handle her skirts to make an audience instantly know she was portraying a woman of the night. Her attention to detail of social body language of the time was key.

Socially Marie was an important figure for young women at a time when a woman's right to speak her mind was debatable. Midge Gillies, in her biography *Marie Lloyd: The One And Only*, describes how young women liked Marie's songs due to her "defiant tone: as well as her glamorous costume". Off-stage it was her seemingly exciting and carefree lifestyle that won approval. A journalist from *The Sketch* who accompanied Marie one evening noted with surprise that: "At the back-door of the varieties, she was presented with a huge cut-glass bottle of scent by a group of East End girls. On the way to Sadlers Wells, another group of girls threw a large box of expensive sweets into the brougham."

Marie's work for charity and her important role in the music hall strike, which paved the way for fair treatment of performers, were documented nearly as well as the gossip about her tumultuous personal life. Three failed marriages (two of which were abusive), a heavy drink problem and party lifestyle can clearly show how she became a fascinating celebrity. Temptress, working class hero and social observer. This was the mix that, inevitably, created the Queen of the Music Hall.

JOSIE LONG (1982-)
By Oliver Double

I first saw Josie Long in 2006 doing a preview of her Edinburgh show *Kindness and Exuberance* at the Horsebridge Centre in Whitstable. It was that night that she broke a snow globe she was using in a routine about finding a linen basket in a charity shop, containing 35 snow globes each of which had a different name on it. The story of the breakage then became part of the show, as she would tell audiences that when it broke, the glitter it had contained had spilled over the floor of the dressing room so that it looked like she had "bled a fairy to death". I'm proud to say I was there on the night that gag was born.

To be honest, I didn't know much about her before going to see Josie that night, except that Stewart Lee was recommending her so she would probably be quite interesting. By the end of the show, I was a committed fan and remain one to this day. What was it about her that immediately struck a chord with me? Strangely enough it was that she came across as being both kind and exuberant.

The natural beat of stand-up is cynicism, so it's surprising and subversive to come across somebody whose comedy is about celebrating things rather than slagging them off. She has those rarest of comic qualities: earnestness and excessive joy. "I have no time for cynicism," she told us that night. "And I don't feel like there's a prize at the end of life. No-one's going to come up to you with a trophy and go, 'Well done! You didn't enjoy any of it!'" Then there's the home-made aspect of her act – giving out little photocopied fanzines before the show, doing routines based on her wonky cartoons felt-tipped onto a dog-eared drawing pad, giving out satsumas to punters who show that they're "trying hard".

A few years down the line, her comedy got a bit angrier, provoked by the awfulness of what's been happening under the baleful rule of the current coalition government. People behaved as if this was a big shift, saying she'd somehow remodeled herself as a political comedian. As far as I could see, it wasn't a shift at all. I interviewed her for a book I was writing and told her I thought she'd always been a political act. "Thank you very much!" she replied, grateful to have been understood. As she puts it, "DIY culture for me is deeply political."

But if I really wanted to sum up why I like Josie Long so much, I'd go back to the snow globes routine. The point is it's about her joy in everyday eccentricity, as she marvels at somebody's intriguing, obsessive hobby. Much of the time she spends on stage, she's bubbling over with enthusiasm for other people and the quirky things they do – and that's what makes her so delightful. If you don't like Josie Long, you don't like life.

JULIA LOUIS-DREYFUS (1961-)
By Paul Duffus

No other comic actor in the history of television has achieved the combined critical and commercial success of Julia Louis-Dreyfus. Across three decades and, significantly, three separate shows, she is arguably the most successful sitcom actor of all time.

The former *Saturday Night Live* cast member is best known for her role as Elaine Benes in *Seinfeld*, the colossus that dominated US TV ratings for much of the 1990s. The character, like the show itself, was a juxtaposition of the very stupid and the very clever. Elaine was smart and beautiful, a college graduate, an apparently successful career woman, and yet something – call it her 'inner idiot' – seemed to sabotage her at every turn. And so here she was, stuck hanging out with three other idiots in a never ending loop of weird boyfriends, even weirder bosses, and trips to the coffee shop. Julia played the role with a perfect mix of charm and spikiness, meaning that while Elaine more than matched George, Jerry and Kramer for selfishness and venality, audiences couldn't help but love this unsympathetic character. It earned her a Golden Globe, an Emmy, and two personal SAG awards.

After the incredible success of *Seinfeld*, it may sound strange to say, but it is perhaps what Julia has done post-Elaine that is even more significant and separates this extraordinary comedian from her peers. Few comic actors get to play an iconic character like Elaine (Lucille Ball or Roseanne Barr, for example), but fewer still, if any, enjoy second or third successes distinct from the role that initially made them. Julia's next successful show, *The New Adventures of Old Christine*, ran from 2005 to 2010 with healthy ratings and yet another Emmy award. Breaking the so-called *Seinfeld Curse*, it was the first and to date only post-*Seinfeld* sitcom success for any of that show's four principals.

Veep, which began in 2012, represents Julia's unprecedented hat-trick. Selina Meyer, the US vice president of the title who stumbles from one omnishambles to another, is a character who simultaneously manages to be both brilliantly successful and disastrously incompetent. For Julia, a skilled clown who in a heartbeat can switch from playing the buffoon to delivering the most acerbic, intelligent, jaw-dropping insults, it is perhaps an even better role than Elaine. Three more Emmys, a SAG Award, and two Critics Choice Awards are testament to this astonishing achievement.

ZOE LYONS (1971-)
By Rosie Wilby

Not many people know this but Zoe and I were at York University at the same time a few (cough) years ago. We didn't know each other well, but crossed paths now and then due to being unrequitedly in lust with the same woman. The woman in question roundly ignored both of us but I was glad to have this connection with Zoe. It gave us something to talk about when we bumped into each other years later at the Edinburgh Fringe in 2002. I was performing as an earnest acoustic songwriter and had not yet contemplated a transition into comedy. She was in a two-hander sketch show, her profile as a jobbing actress having been boosted by an uncharacteristically duplicitous appearance on ITV's *Survivor*.

Then in 2004, when my music career had fatally stalled and my own dalliance with reality TV on E4's *Chained* had merely resulted in me being recognised once (just once!) on the 43 bus, a magically inspiring thing happened. I received an email from Zoe telling me she was doing stand-up and felt like it was exactly what she was meant to be doing. She invited me to see her set at Comedy Camp in Soho. I was immediately impressed by her assured energy delivery as she merrily informed us that she looked like a cross between Cherie Blair and Myra Hindley.

A door of possibility creaked open in my mind that I might like to have a go at this if a woman in her early 30s, not some 18-year-old lad but a real person that I knew, was having so much fun doing it. The atmosphere at the club was an eye-opener, too. It was a gay friendly comedy night. I didn't know such things existed. Sadly Comedy Camp no longer does, but Zoe can be found at the helm of the monthly Bent Double in Brighton, which runs along similar lines.

Zoe went on to win Funny Women in 2004 and reach the finals of So You Think You're Funny. She kept popping up on TV and Radio 4 and was getting busier and busier but was generous enough to recommend a few London gigs to me when I started dipping my own toes in the treacherous comedy waters. I started to feel a bit in awe when I learned it wasn't as effortless as she had made it look. Yet as her award nominations for best newcomer at Edinburgh Fringe in 2007 and best Joke at the Fringe in 2008 kept coming in, it was genuinely inspiring.

Last time we gigged together, she was previewing a new routine prompted by a vision of seeing a very proud woman pushing along two Chihauhaus in a dog pram. No comic mind would let this slip by unnoticed, but few would imbue these tiny dogs with the names, voices, personalities and vivid descriptions Zoe does to perfectly illustrate the absurdity of this invention.

Just go see her, OK?

MIRIAM MARGOLYES (1941-)

By Cerys Nelmes

I have always had two great loves in my life growing up, one is musical theatre and the other is comedy. These two things are the reason I chose to write about one of my favourite ever females, Miriam Margolyes. An actor for nearly 50 years, Miriam started her career as a voice over artist on a soft porn recording! A girl after my own heart.

I first became aware of Miriam while watching *Blackadder* with my dad when I was younger. As one of the few female characters, she stood out as a strong, funny woman that held her own among the men. Always playing slightly weird characters but I guess that was *Blackadder* on the whole.

I then remember seeing her as the dental nurse on *The Little Shop of Horrors* and this became the usual thing. You would catch Miriam playing a supporting character, but to me she was always memorable. She seemed to get typecast, somewhat, again playing a nurse in one of my favourite films *Romeo + Juliet*. I can see why, she has this whole warm maternal thing going on. More and more I'd start to recognise Miriam's voices in favourite family films like *James and the Giant Peach* and *Babe*, and then later on *Happy Feet* and *Flushed Away*, films I would watch with my son. Then along came *Harry Potter* and Miriam was centre stage again.

My favourite ever memory of Miriam was when my son and I went to New York, as a combined birthday treat, for my 30th and his 10th in 2008. I vowed that while we were there we would see at least one musical on Broadway. I knew Miriam was in *Wicked* and this was my first choice of musical. I tried to purchase tickets before we went but as it had only just hit Broadway, tickets were non-existent. This was the case also when we arrived in New York. So off we went to see *Mary Poppins*, which was fabulous, but for the next 10 days I dreamed non-stop of *Wicked*. It was then that our hotel receptionist told us that we could queue for any returned tickets on the night. So that evening this is exactly what we set out to do. We queued and bought tickets for $125 each. The seats were fantastic, Miriam was fabulous and it was the original Broadway cast so we had Idina Menzel and Kristin Chenoweth as well. Worth $250 of anyone's money, I think you'll agree.

More recently Miriam has become a hit with the youngsters after appearing on Graham Norton with Will-i-am. Hilarity ensued in this interview and this can be viewed on YouTube at your pleasure. It was innocent, unaffected, comedic Miriam at her best.

I can sum up my feelings for Miriam Margolyes by saying that watching her is like keeping an eye on a slightly mad aunt! It's things like this that make me love her.

FRANCESCA MARTINEZ (1978-)

Having made her name as a child actor in the long-running TV show *Grange Hill*, Francesca Martinez moved into comedy in the early 2000s – where she was swiftly named as one of the top fifty funniest people in the UK by *The Observer* in 2003.

Francesca was born with cerebral palsy, although she chooses to use the term "wobbly" to describe herself. She has dedicated much of her media profile as a comedian to promoting disability issues and campaign for a fairer welfare system. As such, in November 2013 she delivered a petition with 100,000 signatures on to the government, calling for an end to the cuts to disability provisions. Consequently, in 2014 BBC Radio 4's *Woman's Hour* included Francesca on its Power List.

At the heart of Francesca's comedy and campaigning is the point that there is no such thing as normal, and her successful show and book *What The Fuck Is Normal?* proves just this.

JESSIE MATTHEWS (1907-1981)

In the inter-war period, Jessie Matthews was hot property – not bad for a girl born behind a butcher's shop in Soho, London. Despite being in the middle of 16 children and growing up in relative poverty, Jessie attended dance classes and ultimately won a role as Gertrude Lawrence's understudy in a production of *Review* in 1924 – when Gertrude fell ill during the New York leg of the tour, Jessie was thrust into the limelight… and never looked back.

Back in the UK, Jessie became a hugely popular musical film star thanks to her warm voice and enormously likeable personality, with her saucer-like wide eyes becoming her trademark. In 1937, she was ranked as the third most popular movie star in the UK by *Motion Picture Herald*. Her breakthrough performance was in the 1933 film *The Good Companions*, which led to the 1935 comedy gender-swapping musical comedy *First A Girl*.

In later years, Jessie was the replacement voice for Mary Dale in the BBC's *Mrs Dale's Diary*: the first ever long-running radio serial.

MEL AND SUE (1968-) (1969-)

By Joanne Hollows

While numerous sitcoms have celebrated female friendship, the emotional experience of feminine friendliness is rarely seen to have comic potential. Many female comedians are celebrated for their play with dangerous, grotesque or unruly femininities rather than more ordinary qualities like warmth and intimacy. But Mel and Sue have deployed these very qualities to gently undermine some of the gendered conventions of TV comedy.

Both Mel Giedroyc and Sue Perkins have worked on individual projects. In particular, Sue has feminised the traditionally masculine role of the posh and educated wit found on BBC panel shows, brainy quizzes and esoteric documentaries. However, it is as a double act that Mel and Sue have deployed the humorous patterns of female friendship in their roles as comic presenters.

This dates back to the launch of their TV careers as the hosts of Channel 4's cult daytime chat-and-cooking show *Light Lunch* in the late 1990s. Their repartee with each other was reminiscent of sixth-form grammar school girls, combining silliness, playfulness, bad puns and quips with a substantial dose of gentle self-deprecation. Rather than drawing attention to the specialness of their own comic performance, they used humour to invite those around them – celebrity guests, the studio audience and, by extension, the audience at home – into the fun of their friendship. While this could have led to something rather tepid and safe, instead it enabled Mel and Sue to make little digs at the demands of conventional femininity. Indeed, Sue went on to deploy the power of the grumbling aside in the *Supersizers* series of programmes in which she was partnered with Giles Coren. While sampling the food practices of different historical periods, she muttered about the ridiculous demands various regimes placed on women.

These skills as comic presenters have made Mel and Sue an indispensable part of the BBC's unexpected ratings winner *The Great British Bake Off*. Rather than using comedy performance to compete against the contestants on the show for the viewers' attention, Mel and Sue take the role of the bakers' friends and confidantes and use humour to soothe baking-induced stress. Like ideal friends and family, they happily eat whatever is put in front of them and act on the audience's behalf to defend the contestants from the criticisms of the judges. While many of these same techniques have also been used to great effect by Ant and Dec on shows like *Pop Idol*, female comedy partnerships (at least outside of the sitcom) have rarely been used to anchor prime-time TV. Mel and Sue use the kind of humour that sustains female friendships behind closed doors and circulate it in a very public space.

SARAH MILLICAN (1975-)
By Louise Wingrove

Like many of the nation's favourites, Sarah Millican has shot to success due to her everyday observational comedy. Comedians from the embryonic stages of stand-up, performing on the music hall stage, right up to the constantly evolving and radical comics of today, have realised the importance of using identifiable material to make their audience feel included and understood.

However, her talent is for interspersing sudden shockingly explicit comments, bookended neatly with other comments of domestic wholesomeness. She manages to juggle jokes of self-deprecation and cynicism with a relaxed delivery that still keeps her sets light hearted and this equally makes it more acceptable for her to make fun of others.

No one is safe, not even Sarah herself, but it is all in the best possible taste. Her lyrical Geordie accent and alternating coy/abrupt delivery make her likeable rather than offensive, but her matter-of-fact stance and confident body language make quite sure we know who is in charge.

Part of being able to make an audience relate to you is found through audience interaction. Talking to audience members is important and makes them feel the set is unique for them, but audience interaction is equally about the way everyone is addressed. During her sets, Sarah will constantly address her stories to the people in the front row and will look all around the space and smile at different audience members in different areas of the audience. This ability to seem like she is addressing and welcoming everyone is what gives her sets warmth, and a sense of safety in which to say naughty things without rebuke.

It is said that break-ups make the best material, but since her early sets – which focused on her divorce – Sarah has proved that success and a relationship need not ruin a comedic mind. If her constant presence on our TV screens on panel shows, comedy roadshows and her own series weren't enough to justify her title of The People's Choice: Queen of Comedy (2011), then the fact that her DVD *Chatterbox Live* has sold more copies than that of any other female comedian secures her a particular place in people's homes and no doubt their affections.

MISS PIGGY (1974-)
By Juliette Burton

As a great Muppet once said: "No one makes an entrance like Miss Piggy." She's everything I aspire to be: strong, passionate, confident; a feisty go-getter whose femininity empowers her. She knows who she is, what she wants and stops at nothing to get it. When she walks on stage, she steals the scene.

Like all great women, she's one of a kind. Jim Henson, creator of The Muppets, once said: "…we'd anticipate coming up with new personalities with the same kind of appeal as Kermit, Fozzie or Gonzo. We will not create anybody with Piggy's kind of appeal – nobody should try."

She might not technically be a comedian. I mean she's neither human nor a stand-up. But she's a skilled actress with comedic technique and emotional depth more believable than any Botox-ed film star. And her career has lasted longer, too.

From humble beginnings as a one-dimensional running gag in *The Muppet Show* back in 1976, she's now a multi-faceted, complex character I identify with strongly. Close friend of Piggy, Frank Oz, said of her: "The coyness hiding the aggression, the conflict of love with her desire for a career; her hunger for a glamour image; her tremendous out-and-out ego; all these things are great fun to explore in a character." And all these things are greatly familiar to many women in comedy, like me.

Piggy inspires me to seize the day: she bravely leaves her small-town life to join a frog, a bear and a... Gonzo to head for Hollywood (*The Muppet Movie*), she bends metal bars to break herself and her companions out of prison (*The Great Muppet Cape*r), she overcomes her personal grief to save the day and help her friends (*The Muppets*).

In her most recent movie, Piggy is a powerful Plus Size Editor of *Vogue*. Now, I'm not ashamed to admit I'm a girly girl. I love clothes. I can't afford them, but I love them. Piggy, my hero, doesn't have to worry about paying for her plus-sized garments: she's a fashion muse! In 2012, she was dressed by Zac Posen for the Oscars, Marc Jacobs for the BAFTAs and in her role of editor she wears a custom-made Chanel suit. Jason Wu, Giles Deacon, Michael Kors; leading designers are clamouring to dress her fabulous fuller figure.

Since skeletal fashion models are still held as examples of womanhood, we need starlets like Miss Piggy who dress to celebrate all that they have, all that they are and never hide away.

Most importantly she's a central character in a larger group that helped thousands of people, young and old, to laugh for nearly four decades (and somehow she's never aged. Maybe she did have Botox...).

The Muppets show me how important it is to be a part of something bigger than myself, to be connected, to belong. They're misfits who belong together. And in comedy, being a misfit counts for a lot.

NANCY MITFORD (1904-1973)

The eldest of the legendary Mitford sisters, like her six siblings Nancy was a renowned socialite and close friend of the writer Evelyn Waugh. Encouraged by Evelyn, Nancy started writing novels as a means to supplement the comparatively small allowance her father gave her. Her sharp wit and satires of the social lives of the upper classes made her an enormously popular novelist, particularly with books such as *The Pursuit Of Love* (1945), *Love In A Cold Climate* (1948), which were loose depictions of events and characters within her own family.

In the early 1940s Nancy began working at the Heywood Hill bookshop on London's Curzon Street (still operating today) – and the shop subsequently became a central meeting point for London's literati of the time.

"If one can't be happy, one must be amused – don't you agree?" Nancy once wrote to a friend, which is a simple line that explains her philosophy on life. With a string of failed relationships and unsuccessful attempts to become a mother, Nancy continued to be amused by life and to make others laugh with what she wrote.

MABEL NORMAND (1892-1930)

A stalwart of the Keystone Studios, American actor and comedian Mabel Normand was one of the big stars of the silent era. She was only 16 when she entered the world of movies, and by the age of 18 she had the lead part in director DW Griffiths' short film *Her Awakening*, which brought Mabel new attention and catapulted her into the spotlight.

Mabel regularly appeared in comedy films alongside the likes of Charlie Chaplin and Fatty Arbuckle, and on occasion she wrote and directed her own films in which she cast Charlie as her lead. Indeed, Charlie's famous Tramp character was first spotted in *Mabel's Strange Predicament* (1914). Mabel and Charlie maintained a close friendship after she helped him overcome his initial difficulties with the transition from switching between the demands of music hall stage acting and Hollywood film acting… a move that didn't initially come naturally to him.

Mabel was only 37 when she died in 1930 after a long illness with tuberculosis. She is immortalised with a star on the Hollywood Walk Of Fame.

DOROTHY PARKER (1893-1967)
By Amy Mason

The first time I heard of Dorothy Parker was as a Sylvia Plath worshipping 17 year old. My much-loved grandma was the giver, but it took me a while to get round to reading it. A glance at the cover showed that it was 'comic' writing from the 1920s and 1930s. I couldn't imagine I would enjoy it – preoccupied as I was at the time with self-harm, getting off with boys, and drinking cider and black.

I'm not sure when I first actually read it. I can imagine though. Me, lying on my top bunk, skiving off exams, sobbing along to the Manic Street Preachers, desperate and furious, my arms freshly scratched with a razor blade, drafting suicide notes in the back of my rough book.

And then, bored, I flicked open the book my grandma had just given me. Perhaps it was *Résumé* I read first, or *Symptom Recital*. Whatever it was, I was confronted with a woman who properly understood me. She hated her appearance! She wanted to die! Boys never called her back either! But... she was funny. And unlike Sylvia, despite her obsession with suicide, she lived to be 73.

Rereading Dorothy now, her work seems to be dripping with the white privilege so often leveled at writers like Lena Dunham. Indeed, Dorothy's first collection was dismissed by the *New York Times* as "flapper verse", and it would be easy to see her as nothing more than a rich white girl making superficial and mean remarks.

In fact, Dorothy knew this better than anyone and the spite of her verse (and perhaps her life-long battle with booze) was driven in part by her self-loathing. She hated being called a "wise-cracker" and later denigrated the Algonquin Round Table group of writers (which she had helped found) for its frivolity.

But there was always far more to her than expensive lunches and spiteful wisecracks. After moving to Hollywood to pursue a lucrative screenwriting career, she was eventually blacklisted as a communist, having founded the Hollywood Anti-Nazi League and campaigned avidly for civil rights. Dorothy left her entire estate to Dr Martin Luther King Jr, and her remains lie outside the National Advancement of Association for Colored People in Baltimore, with the epitaph (of her choosing) "excuse my dust".

Dorothy Parker taught me that you can be angry and funny, jilted and funny… you can even be suicidal and funny. Most importantly of all, she taught me that I might as well live.

JOAN RIVERS (1933-2014)
By Paul Duffus

No American comedian in the history of stand-up worked for longer and with as much success as Joan Rivers. For a combination of longevity and popularity, she out-shone everyone.

Create an imaginary pantheon of American stand-up comedians. Richard Pryor, George Carlin, Woody Allen? She outlived the first two and, as a stand-up, out-worked all three. Jackie Mason? He surpasses Joan for longevity by perhaps less than a decade and counting, but did he ever have his own late night talk show? In 1986 Joan became the first woman to do just this, a remarkable achievement in a field still dominated by male stand-ups. Aside from Jackie Mason, there's really no-one else even close. If this fanciful all-star stand-up team had been drafted in 2013, Bill Cosby would have been first pick as the only comedian to match Joan. Now as his legacy unravels, Joan stands apart from all her peers.

Over her five decades of live work and numerous TV shows, stand-up albums and stand-up specials, Joan pioneered a style of stand-up that was abrasive, personal and often aggressive. Whether making jokes about herself, social mores, public figures, or any other subject, she held nothing back. In the 1960s she shocked audiences with jokes about sex, speaking with a frankness that at the time was shocking for a female comedian. Fifty years later, she shocked audiences with jokes about 9/11, still speaking with an impudence and fearlessness to put most younger comedians to shame.

GINGER ROGERS (1911-1995)

By Andrew Kelly

Film lovers all have their favourite film moments. In *The Moviegoer*, Walker Percy says "The fact is I am quite happy in a movie, even a bad movie".

Other people, so I have read, treasure memorable moments in their lives: the time one climbed the Parthenon at sunrise, the summer night one met a lonely girl in Central Park and achieved with her a sweet and natural relationship, as they say in books. I too once met a girl in Central Park, but it is too much to remember. What I remember is the time John Wayne killed three men with a carbine as he was falling to the dusty street in *Stagecoach*, and the time the kitten found Orson Welles in the doorway in *The Third Man*.

I remember these moments – as I remember Jean Simmons singing in *The Way To The Stars* and Ginger Rogers dancing the *Black Bottom* in *Roxie Hart*.

Before the play and film *Chicago* there was *Roxie Hart*, itself based on a 1920s play. Roxie, a fading showgirl, admits to killing a man found in her husband's apartment to save her career. In 1920s Chicago women were rarely convicted of murder – Billy Flynn, Roxie's flamboyant lawyer, says "the law doesn't count. It's justice we're after". She gets the press on side (not hard); feigns pregnancy when her case flags; and eventually gets off by charming the jury members.

The film has it all – a venal press, corrupt lawyers, a judge keen on getting into the papers (every time a picture is taken in the court room he stands in the background); an ensemble cast where each person plays a role or has something significant to say; and Ginger Rogers, a wisecracking, gallery-playing, people-using, gum-chewing, leg-showing, street fighting bad women. In jail she is persuaded to do her signature dance, the *Black Bottom* and, in a glorious Hollywood three minutes, she gets the whole cell to join in – newspaper reporters, society columnist, waiter, jailor, maid and more.

Ginger had depth: dancer, serious actress, comedy star. In *Roxie Hart* she was at her best. Like all films it took a group to make a classic: Adolphe Menjou as Billy Flynn never better; Phil Silvers in plus-fours as a photographer brilliant; Sara Allgood and Spring Byngton dance the *Black Bottom* with gusto. William Wellman's crisp direction helped create 75 minutes of joy. And Ginger Rogers at the centre – what a film and what a star.

JOANNA SCANLAN (1961-)

By Ian Martin

No comedy performer in the world does 'bumptious' better than Joanna Scanlan. She is the Queen of Bumptiousness. Truly Bumptious.

Of course she's a brilliant actress with a full spectrum of character skills. It's just that when she puts on that look of purse-lipped, repressed irritability, she's invincible.

I remember in 2009 being in a cinema watching *In The Loop* when she appeared as the disconnected constituency agent Roz, chivvying Tom Hollander's disdainful MP into a dismal surgery. You could feel the relaxed murmur rippling like a Mexican Wave through the audience: oh good, it's Jo Scanlan doing her 'face'.

I've always had a bit of a comedy crush on Jo, and I welcome this chance to fly the flag for her queenly talent. It's not that she's underrated as a comedy actor; mention her name and people go "oh yeah she's amazing isn't she, I liked her years before anyone else, did you see her in *Spaced*, you know what's really great about her is the way she taps into humanity itself, it's like she's Everywoman or rather Everyperson, know what I mean, you can see it in that conflict of self-doubt and defiance she plays so well, that articulation through comedy of the human condition itself…" and then you tell them to shut up, while mentally filing this observation away to use later. She's definitely isn't underrated, but I think she definitely is taken for granted a bit.

Which is ironic I suppose, given the roles she's best known for. In both *The Thick of It* and *Getting On*, she plays characters in thankless jobs with patronising superiors. As Terri Coverley in *The Thick Of It* she was an arse-covering civil servant trapped in a minor government department with disdainful, incompetent colleagues, and a carousel of fiercely tribal yet indistinguishable politicians. As Den Flixter in *Getting On* she was a beleaguered ward sister trapped in an under-resourced NHS geriatric ward, under pressure from the job. And from disdainful and incompetent colleagues, again.

I was lucky enough to see Jo being brilliant close up, on *The Thick Of It* set. On that last series there were quite a few women being brilliant. Somehow, though, Terri was the only one I ever felt sorry for. A bit guilty, even. We were writing one episode, inventing cruel taunts for the other characters to lob at Terri, who has put on her slap for the arrival of then Opposition secretary of state Peter Mannion ("Peter Man-Yum"). I told Jo I felt uncomfortable, as if I was empowering bullies. I think she thought, quite rightly, I was a bit soft.

Then Mannion's lot took over at DoSAC and he was just as horrible. Him and his junior Coalition partners. No wonder jobsworth Terri switched off all work devices at 6pm: "After that it's just me, the Kindle and Jodi Picoult..." I challenge any actor to make that sound anywhere near as funny. Some lines can make you laugh off the page. "TERRI (tapping bluetooth) Coverley, Comms". I'm smiling now, just seeing her do it.

And then. To co-write and co-star in *Getting On*! A comedy so dark it's pitch black. Every joke in the bleakness a star in the night sky. I cannot shake the image of a wronged Den, pissed, her make-up ruined, articulating once again the human condition, as promised earlier.

When *Getting On* first aired, the papers were full of stories about women "breaking through", and "reshaping comedy". Sadly, they were mostly talking about *Miranda*. I genuinely have nothing against Miranda Hart. If I had young children who found it funny I'm sure I'd be very fond of it. But a female character who's childishly, flailingly incompetent? Who pines for the man who will 'complete her'? Quite how that advances the cause is a mystery. *Getting On* pushed 'women in comedy' forward by miles, and STILL remains cult viewing.

I mentioned Jo on Twitter and instantly got two warm responses. The first was from a former drama student who'd been taught by Jo and remembered her infinite calmness, encouragement and patience. "She once conducted a seminar in the lotus position."

The second was from Ben Willbond, who played Adam in *The Thick Of It*. He mentioned David Mamet's ideas about technique in acting. "He talks about listening, because that's what you do when someone talks to you: you listen then respond. That's what people mean when they say someone is generous. It means that they are doing their job. Jo, as an actor, listens." It's why, Ben says, Jo's so good at improv. "She'll do something different each take because she's reacting differently to your performance. Because she's listening."

So I propose a toast on behalf of all of us to Joanna Scanlan, comedy genius, who IS all of us.

SARAH SILVERMAN (1970-)

By Paul Duffus

"Kind of Jewy but totally hot — not out-of-your-league hot, just cute."

The description of Sarah Silverman given by a convenience store clerk in the second episode of her eponymous sitcom, a self-description by proxy, captures the main features of the Silverman comic persona: obnoxious self-regard, a dumb lack of self-awareness, and an apparent obliviousness to decorum, sensitivity and political correctness. A phrase like "kind of Jewy" with its racial stereotyping would be outré for some comedians, even self-directed as it is, but on the Silverman Scale of Offensiveness the needle barely moves.

Her best known stand-up special *Jesus is Magic* is a cataclysm of material about the Holocaust, rape and 9/11, among other things, lovingly knitted together with songs full of racial stereotypes and dying pensioners. The whole set is delivered with trademark vanity, a big grin and, most importantly of all, a dead earnestness. This last thing, the absolute sincerity with which she delivers this earth-scorching material, is why we love Sarah Silverman, why she's one of the most famous stand-up comedians in the world, and why she's the defining stand-up of her age. When we look back the late 1990s/2000s, Sarah will be one of comedians we remember.

Sarah's satire of the US right wing and clumsy leftwing guilt depends on her ability to fully sell the audience on her character's utter stupidity. Lesser comedians might employ irony as a Trojan horse, a delivery system to inveigle potentially offensive material into the mainstream. However, what sets Sarah apart is her apparent lack of irony. She may in reality be an Obama-loving left wing stoner, but on stage not for one second can the audience know this. Other comedians may tell a rape joke and then wink to let everyone know that they don't mean it. Sarah just smiles. She really did mean it. In the context of her act, with its the dumb narcissism and occasionally surreal flights of nonsense, what could be gratuitous and nothing more than an attempt to appeal to genuine irony-immune lovers of rape jokes becomes satire of that very mindset.

Her skill as an actress is attested to by a long list of TV and films credits. Her TV work in particular includes some of the most canonical comedy shows of their day, including *Mr Show*, *The Larry Sanders Show* and *Seinfeld*. Her own sitcom ran for three seasons. It is onstage though with her perfect veneer of shock and idiocy – fashioned with acute intelligence – where Sarah's acting skills are best represented.

CARLY SMALLMAN (1985-)
By James Mullinger

Like most people, I first saw Carly Smallman perform when she appeared on BBC's *The Rob Brydon Show* in 2010. My first thought was: "Why the hell haven't I heard of this act before?" I had been performing on the stand-up circuit for five years and here was this awesome comedian I hadn't even heard of performing on a prime time chat show hosted by a national treasure.

My surprise (translation: jealousy) was short lived as I started doing something I rarely do when watching comedy on television. I howled with laughter. Uncontrollable, unable to breathe belly laughs. Singing *Romantic Love Song* she somehow made a song about incest hilarious. And hilarious to a primetime audience. The word is overused but I remember thinking: "Genius".

I couldn't hate this person for being all famous on telly and stuff while I was still playing grotty pubs because she was clearly a unique and brilliant talent. I watched her performance again on BBC iPlayer and laughed just as hard. Then I showed my wife who laughed even more. Today I watched it again to research this piece and posted it on Facebook. My sister-in-law emailed me within minutes saying how marvellous it is.

Four months later I was compering a gig for Off The Kerb at Reading University. I was delighted to discover that Carly was headlining the gig. Before the show I was outside smoking and she walked up carrying her guitar and asked me for a light. Now here's the thing. I feel nervous about meeting anyone I admire. So even though I am almost a decade older than her and had been performing considerably longer, I was shy. Yes, I am pathetic but there you have it. I didn't know what to say other than, "I think you are awesome". But she was the epitome of charm and we shared almost as many laughs puffing snouts as she got on stage that night when she absolutely stormed the gig.

Since that time we have toured together all around the country and become good friends. She has witnessed me being stopped by the police for "erratic driving". She has also witnessed me get up on stage after accidentally drinking six Red Stripes and 12 jager bombs.

People often ask you what is the best thing about being a comedian. Obviously the buzz of performing comes high on the list. You couldn't do this job full of rejection and self-loathing unless you really, really love the art form. I guess that some comedians enjoy groupies although I have never met one. A groupie that is. I've met loads of comedians who sleep around. The best thing really about being a comedian is that you get to become friends with those you admire. Growing up I worshipped comedians that I saw on TV. Joan Rivers. Frank Skinner. French and Saunders. If I were 11 years old now, I would have watched Carly Smallman and wished that one day I would meet her.

And I continue to be impressed by her. Her Edinburgh show in 2013, *The Appalling Carly Smallman,* was an absolute riot. She is a joy to watch. And it is not an exaggeration to say that she is probably one of my Top Ten favourite comedians of all time. You can just hear the bores now: "But what about Pryor, Hicks, etc". Hey, I know what I like. Comedy, like food, is subjective. I've never understood why people always question your comedy choices like they know better. No-one ever questions the choice of last supper made by a death row prisoner. "Really? You want spaghetti bolognaise? What about a chicken kiev because that's my favourite." "Erm, I'm the one dying tonight, I'll choose what I want thank you very much."

So in short, I know what makes me laugh hysterically, makes me happy and makes me love life. It ain't Hicks or Pryor. It's Smallman.

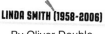

LINDA SMITH (1958-2006)
By Oliver Double

I was lucky enough to know Linda Smith personally. Back in the 1980s, we were both part of what might laughably be called the Sheffield alternative comedy scene. There were no more than about eight of us, and when I first met her, Linda was the only one with a proper career. She had already built quite a following in the city, and was regularly going down to perform in London where the new comedy was really happening. I was just some jumped up new kid on the block, full of youthful arrogance, but she talked to me like an equal and answered my questions with care and consideration.

There were people she was less polite to. Politicians generally, and Tories in particular, were often the target of the barbed wit she so expertly wielded in her stand-up act. Not that she was some kind of furious ranter. She always came across as down-to-earth and perfectly reasonable as she skewered the targets of her satire, and had a gift for summing up her anger at the injustice of the world with a well-turned phrase. Commenting on the cutbacks of the Thatcher era, she'd cheerfully pipe up with, 'I don't like this new fun-sized NHS, do you?' Sometimes the put-downs would be aimed at particular people. She described John Major as "slightly less popular than Hezbollah", and David Blunkett as "Satan's bearded folk singer".

Linda's act was about more than just politics though, and her comedy betrayed her childhood growing up in a small town and having to find ways to amuse herself. She was hilariously vitriolic about her home town of Erith, saying it was so boring that "it's not twinned with anywhere – but it does have a suicide pact with Dagenham". She was an expert at comic imagery. Discussing the habit of young northerners going out clubbing on a winter night without a coat, she hypothesised that they could use their goose pimples to grate nutmeg.

I didn't hear about her for a while after she'd left Sheffield for London, but then she started turning up on those old warhorses of BBC radio comedy, *Just A Minute* and *The News Quiz*. She'd clearly found her natural home on Radio 4, getting her own series and being voted 'Wittiest Living Person' by the station's listeners.

A few years down the line, I turned on the radio in the car on the way home from work and it was in the middle of what was clearly a news report about somebody's death. As I listened to the nice things people were saying about the person I started trying to work out who had died. Before I'd even left the car park, I realised with a chill that it was Linda.

In 2013, her partner Warren Lakin passed on a massive archive of her scripts and private recordings to the University of Kent, where I work. I'm proud that we'll be able to use it to preserve her memory.

CONSTANCE TALMADGE (1898-1973)

Silent movie star Constance Talmadge was the middle of three acting sisters who stole the hearts of Hollywood. Constance told a *PhotoPlay* journalist in 1917: "At home, we used to play show in the cellar and we made mother come as audience, and when she didn't like the show we'd lock her in so she'd have to stay!" This wicked sense of humour set Constance up for life.

Where Constance differed was that she was the sibling with true star value and the funniest bones. Not one to be seen as a weak woman, in the 1916 DW Griffiths film *Intolerance* Constance was left with black and blue bruises all over her legs as a result of insisting on driving a chariot led by huge galloping horses herself (she later joked to a journalist that she was going to get herself a horse-drawn chariot to go out and do her shopping in). And it was this feisty, can-do attitude that propelled her into the world's hearts.

Writer Antia Loos adored Constance's casual attitude to life, and wrote a string of screenplays for her friend including the comedies *A Virtuous Vamp* (1919) and *Woman's Place* (1921). Constance maintained that she preferred subtle, gentle comedy to the blunt, slapstick style of comedy, and stuck to her guns by appearing in more than 80 movies during the course of her career.

Constance was at the peak of her career when she starred in the feature-length *Her Sister From Paris* in 1925, in a classic case of mistaken identity. This is one of Constance's few surviving films, and is an excellent showcase for her comic timing and performance. When the talkies began to dominate Hollywood in the late 1920s, Constance's movie career was over and she sadly succumbed to a retirement of failed marriages and substance abuse.

SUE TOWNSEND (1946-2014)

As the author of the hugely popular Adrian Mole diary series, writer Sue Townsend created a character that personified self-absorbed 1980s' angst, the excesses of 1990s' wealth, and the depression of 2000s' over-indulgence. During the 1980s, the Adrian Mole books sold more than any other work of fiction published that decade, and despite being satirical tomes they still stand up as good reference points for remembering how people were thinking –

whether or not they'd like to admit it – back in those murky decades that aren't as long ago as we might choose to acknowledge

Sue's other satirical novels, including *The Queen and I* (1992) and *The Woman Who Went To Bed For A Year* (2012), were also bestsellers, but it is for Adrian Mole that she will be best remembered. More than 10 million copies of her books have been sold in the UK alone, and that figure keeps rising each year.

TRACEY ULLMAN (1959-)

By Viv Groskop

Tracey Ullman was the best thing to happen to comedy in the early 1980s. I was nearly ten years old and she was the greatest thing I had ever seen, heard or even imagined. The real star of sketch show *Three Of A Kind* (next to Lenny Henry and David Copperfield), she soon went to Hollywood as the host of *The Tracey Ullman Show*. The series won loads of Emmys, spawned *The Simpsons* and gave Paula Abdul a career (as resident choreographer). But we cannot hold Tracey responsible for that. Tracey became one of the most successful and wealthiest entertainers in the world.

Tracey was the first female comic who wasn't a fictional character who I found funny – and also moving. Her talent was (and is) immense. I frequently dreamed she was my best friend. It helped that she bore a close physical resemblance to my Auntie Lynne (who was often asked to impersonate Tracey and would obligingly sing a few bars of her hit song *They Don't Know About Us*). I always thought that this was a sign: I was related to someone who virtually *was* Tracey Ullman. It meant that one day somehow Tracey and I would be together. It only took 30 years.

The moral of this story is: Do meet your idols. But maybe prepare what you are going to say. A couple of years ago I was at the launch of the *Huffington Post UK*. Tracey Ullman is a friend of the website's founder Arianna Huffington, who I had interviewed that same day. Because I did not know the two of them were friends, it was not the reason why I had gone to the party. I had gone for the free drink. And because I hoped Arianna might say something more controversial than what she had said during the interview, which had mostly been spent in the two of us admiring each other's statement necklaces.

But as soon as I saw Tracey Ullman standing next to the bar, talking very loudly as if she had just stepped out of an episode of *Three Of A Kind*, I transformed into an Exocet missile. I had only dreamed of this day and never believed it would really come. We were going to meet.

I was determined, unstoppable but also strangely silent. I am never, ever starstruck around anyone and even less rarely stuck for words. But next to The Ullman I became one of the yellow minions in *Despicable Me* and could only make unintelligible squeaking noises.

It was the moment in life when I most understood the point of the camera phone. Where words and social interaction and allegedly having a brain failed me, the universal language of the selfie stepped in to save the day. The only other thing I remember about this out-of-body experience is the hilarious, beautiful and profound statement Tracey Ullman uttered to me, now her closest friend in all the world: "I really like your necklace."

JULIE WALTERS (1950-)
By Jayde Adams

When I was little lady, I wanted to be someone else. I was the youngest of three and everyone was kind of past being excited by children but all I wanted was attention. Of an evening, the whole family would sit in front of the TV and watch our favourite shows on full stomachs, normally after a large roast dinner my mum cooked. My parents brought me up on roast dinners and British comedy. I remember watching a lot of women on TV growing up, it's no wonder that I chose comedy as a career. My favourite of all the shows that we watched were shows like *Absolutely Fabulous*, *French and Saunders*, *Smack The Pony* and pretty much anything Victoria Wood wrote. Which meant that her sidekick Julie Walters was a staple part of my TV viewing as a child.

Victoria Wood and Julie Walters were the pinnacle of comedy for me, and Julie in particular was my idol. Every week I'd watch Julie unrecognisably morph into someone else and command a room full of people into hysterical laughter. Myself and my family would fall about crying and snotting on the living room carpet as she became Mrs Overall and various other grotesque creations.

After her shows, my sister and I would disappear to the upstairs bathroom, having stolen my dad's camcorder, and make character driven adverts. Imagine a 10-year-old doing an impression of Julie as Petula Gordino (*Dinner Ladies*). It was awful and I hope we've burned the tapes.

As a child, my sister and I disco danced across the country in sequined lycra. If you don't know what disco dancing is, imagine competitive dance and flexible stick insects dressed in luminous rhinestones. Dancing was the only form of expression I had at that point but it involved me pretending that I was athletic and serious. I didn't want to be beautiful and pretty on stage, that wasn't funny – I wanted to make people laugh like Julie did.

I suppose what I like the most about Julie was she seemed normal, confident and people loved her. She has been an inspiration to me all the way through my life.

It was in the 1970s when Julie had her first break, around a time when funny women on TV were hard to come by. Julie is such a good performer that people forget about insignificant aspects of her like her gender and immerse themselves into whatever character she is performing. That is a sign of a good performer. Someone who can transform themselves unrecognisably and make just about anyone laugh.

RUBY WAX (1953-)

There's not much that American comedian and writer Ruby Wax cannot do. She trained as a serious actor and worked with the Royal Shakespeare Company in the late 1970s and early 1980s. But found a niche as an over-the-top American comic interviewer in London during the early 1980s when the alternative comedy scene was emerging. She quickly hooked up with fellow emerging stars Dawn French, Jennifer Saunders and Tracey Ullman, and the group appeared in two series of the sitcom *Girls On Top*, which first aired in 1985.

Ruby's friendship with Jennifer Saunders was cemented in the early 1980s and the two have continued to work together on a huge range of projects, most notably Jennifer's phenomenally popular sitcom *Absolutely Fabulous*, for which Ruby was script editor as well as an occasional actor.

In more recent years, Ruby has unwittingly become the poster girl for mental illness after her friend, the film director and Comic Relief co-founder Richard Curtis, asked her to help out on a campaign to raise awareness for depression. Suddenly, Ruby was catapulted to a wider audience for something other than her comedy. She has embraced this new responsibility and written several books, including *Sane New World*, to explore the issues of mental health and mindfulness, as well as touring a handful of shows to sell-out audiences where she talks frankly, and amusingly, about her experiences with clinical depression.

BETTY WHITE (1922-)

The grand dame of TV comedy, Betty White is also the only surviving member of the four *Golden Girls*. Long may Betty's star shine, because this is one lady who isn't afraid to stick two fingers up to the industry and go her own way. Betty is one game bird.

Born in Illinois, USA, Betty made history by becoming one of the very first women to have a career not only in front of the TV cameras but also behind it. She's also gone a long way to prove that age doesn't need to be a barrier to success for women. In 2013 the Guinness Book of Records celebrated the fact she had the longest career of any woman working in the entertainment industry. Not only this, but in 2010 Betty became the oldest ever presenter of *Saturday Night Live* (a role for which she won one of her five Emmys), and in 2012 she was the oldest ever recipient of a Grammy Award. And thanks to her nine decades in the spotlight, Betty has more lifetime achievement awards than might be considered decent.

However, it wasn't always this way. In the 1930s, Hollywood rejected Betty because they considered her un-photogenic. So instead she forged a career on radio, hosting *The Betty White Show* in the 1940s… but by the end of that decade she was starting to get small roles on other people's TV shows. Ever the canny businesswoman, in 1952 Betty set up her own production company to make the comedy sketch show *Life With Elizabeth*, in which she played the title role. National syndication of the show led to Betty being one of very few women with a controlling role both in front of and behind the camera.

What ensued was her own TV talk show, film roles, yet more television and recurring work on the legendary *Mary Tyler Moore Show* from the 1970s. Betty never stopped working, but 1985 led to the role for which she is surely most famous – dippy Rose Nylund in long-running NBC sitcom *The Golden Girls*. The show focused on four single, older women who shared a house in Miami and their love lives, friendships and daily dilemmas. If that sounds soppy and dreary, you'd be wrong. The show covered topics ranging from lesbian love, ageism, HIV/AIDS, prescription drug addiction, homelessness and Chronic Fatigue Syndrome. That might not sound much now, but put yourself in a 1985 mindset and think again. For her role as Rose, Betty was the only cast member to be nominated for the Emmy Award for Outstanding Actress In A Comedy Series (and she won the award for the show's first series).

Although *The Golden Girls* came to an end in 1992, Betty's career was far from over. Even though she was 70 years old when she show finished, Betty went on to guest in everything from *Ally McBeal* to *The Ellen Show* and *Friends* spin-off *Joey*. She won yet more Emmy awards, she appeared in Hollywood films, and above all – she has never been afraid to send herself up, even appearing in an *Ugly Betty* spoof called *Ugly Betty White*.

JUNE WHITFIELD (1925-)

Is it fair to say that June Whitfield is the British Betty White? Yes, I'd say so. There's no classic radio or TV show that June hasn't had a part in: from *Hancock's Half Hour*, *Steptoe And Son*, *The Goodies*, *Terry And June*, *Absolutely Fabulous* and *Friends,* to barely scratch the surface of June's impressive filmography.

Back in 1994, June was awarded the Lifetime Achievement Award at the Comedy Awards, but she's showing no signs of slowing down in the two decades since then, despite now being close to the age of 90. And she isn't restricted to comedy roles either, having recently taken parts in cult sci-fi show *Doctor Who* and classic soap opera *Coronation Street*. If there is any better example than June of how we should all aspire to be as we approach our tenth decade, then I can't think of who it is!

In an interview in 2014, June said of the aging process: "The worst thing about age is not quite being able to do what you once did. The best thing is learning to accept what you've got and what you are [28]."

KRISTIN WIIG (1973-)

Kristin Wiig is a genius at creating female comedy characters that may appear confident but are still falling apart at the seams. And there is no better example than her character Annie in the 2011 huge film *Bridesmaids*, which she co-wrote with Annie Mumolo. But Kristin had been a figure on the comedy scene long before *Bridesmaids* catapulted her onto the global screen.

Cutting her teeth on *Saturday Night Live*, Kristin has continued to show no fear about adopting all manner of unsightly prosthetics in order to win some laughs. Whether as a frumpy religious fundamentalist in the Simon Pegg movie *Paul* (2011), or a socially awkward misfit in *Anchor Man 2* (2013), and a hundred other roles, Kristin in not afraid to goof up. And she has also donned some impressive prosthetic-wear to pull off impressions ranging from Bjork to Liza Minnelli.

VICTORIA WOOD (1953-)

By Steven Baxter

We all have our own laughs – some are shrieking, some are roars, some are wails, some are staccato bursts of sound, some are Muttley-like wheezes of air that blast out into the air whether we like it or not. My mother's laugh is something that I still carry around with me. I learned to laugh by watching her.

Sure, she would laugh politely at other TV shows, but there was one thing that made her dissolve into helpless laughter – a kind of silent rocking that made you wonder if she was crying or couldn't breathe, until you saw the tears falling down her face and the giant smile. That programme was *Victoria Wood: As Seen on TV*.

As the only female in a household of four, it wasn't easy for my mother to get control of the TV viewing, but that was the only red line she enforced in our viewing habits. We only had one TV in those days, a battered old wood-effect unit we rented from the shop down the road, but it had four channels and Ceefax, so what else did we need?

I wouldn't miss it either, because it meant I got to spend time with my mum and see her totally at peace, away from the stresses of ordinary life, or children, or work, or anything... I just remember the sense of pure escape in her that only great comedy can bring. And so began my own love of Victoria Wood's comedy.

Here was the first programme I think I'd ever seen where women were in charge. Here was a fictional world of women's television, satirising daytime enforced jolliness like *Pebble Mill* or *Afternoon Plus* while putting females front and centre.

Victoria was leading this programme, with her own stand-up in a ten-sizes-too-big jacket that was adult, bold, uncompromising – slightly too risqué for me to understand at the time, but it made my mother blushingly laugh so I knew I'd return to it one day. She was also generous enough to give some of the best bits to the terrific supporting cast: Susie Blake was the deliciously waspy continuity announcer, chucking verbal hand grenades, and then there was Julie Walters, turning in comic tours de force as the "two soups" waitress or Mrs Overall in *Acorn Antiques*.

Victoria was allowed to be funny. Not token funny or funny in addition to men, but *funny* funny. Take it or leave it, no compromises, this is a woman being funny. It's hard at a distance to take that in, but it was a massive deal. It still is.

That, and she gave me the pleasure, as a small child, of seeing my mother helpless with laughter, submitting to tears of joy. And I will never forget that.

ENDNOTES

01 http://madamjmo.blogspot.co.uk/2012/09/stop-gender-apartheid-of-women-only.html

02 Kohen, Yael, *We Killed* (Picador, 2013), p173

03 http://www.independent.co.uk/arts-entertainment/comedy/features/comedian-jenny-collier-sexism-i-experienced-on-standup-circuit-should-be-extinct-9268417.html?origin=internalSearch

04 Kohen, Yael, *We Killed* (Picador, 2013), p212

05 http://www.bathcomedy.com/vision

06 http://madamjmo.blogspot.co.uk/2012/01/why-is-sarah-millican-minority.html

07 http://gawker.com/here-is-sarah-silvermans-rape-joke-1472012603

08 http://www.chortle.co.uk/correspondents/2012/10/02/16246/women_or_rape%3A_which_is_the_less_funny%3F

09 Horowitz, Susan – *Queens of Comedy* (Routledge, 1997), p17

10 http://www.vanityfair.com/culture/features/2007/01/hitchens200701

11 Kohen, Yael, *We Killed* (Picador, 2013), p180

12 Fey, Tina, *Bossypants* (Sphere, 2011), p144

13 https://www.youtube.com/watch?v=G-w-3CplMi4

14 Horowitz, Susan – *Queens of Comedy* (Routledge, 1997), p4

15 Bevis, Matthew – *Comedy: A Very Short Introduction* (Oxford University Press, 2013), p8

16 Bevis, Matthew – *Comedy: A Very Short Introduction* (Oxford University Press, 2013), p78

17 Horowitz, Susan – *Queens of Comedy* (Routledge, 1997), p4

18 http://artsbeat.blogs.nytimes.com/2008/09/15/whats-the-funniest-novel-ever/?_php=true&_type=blogs&_r=0

19 Kohen, Yael, *We Killed* (Picador, 2013), p192

20 Kohen, Yael, *We Killed* (Picador, 2013), p200

21 Kohen, Yael, *We Killed* (Picador, 2013), p202

22 Brand, Jo, *Can't Stand Up For Sitting Down* (Headline, 2011), p7

23 http://www.theguardian.com/lifeandstyle/2011/apr/16/kathy-burke-interview

24 Ephron, Nora, *Heartburn* (Virago, 2004), pvii

25 http://www.theguardian.com/books/2007/jun/02/uk.hay2007authors

26 http://www.theguardian.com/books/2013/dec/20/bridget-jones-effect-life-thirtysomething-single-woman

27 http://www.theguardian.com/books/2013/apr/21/marian-keyes-depression-mercy-close-interview

28 http://www.telegraph.co.uk/health/dietandfitness/11011167/June-Whitfield-Ive-hired-a-personal-trainer-at-88.html

BIOGRAPHIES OF CONTRIBUTORS

JAYDE ADAMS is the winner of Funny Women 2014 and the London Cabaret Awards 2014. She has been running a successful comedy and cabaret night in London since 2011 and is a popular MC on the cabaret and comedy circuits. Jayde has been What The Frock!'s resident MC since January 2013.

STEVEN BAXTER is a journalist, blogger and writer. He began his journalism career at the turn of the century working for a host of local newspapers, finally becoming a writer and blogger for the *New Statesman*.

JULIETTE BURTON is an award-winning actor, writer and ex-BBC broadcast journalist. Her five-star docu-comedies *When I Grow Up* and *Look At Me* have been huge hits at the comedy festivals. Juliette is working on TV/web shows and a new live show.

MIRANDA DAWE is an actor and singer who started performing comedy in 2012 after participating on Logan Murray's comedy course. She appeared in the sketch show Newsrevue and was a semi-finalist in the Funny Women Awards 2013.

OLIVER DOUBLE used to be a comedian and run comedy clubs, and has written a number of books and articles about stand-up and popular performance. He now works in the drama department at the University of Kent, where he teaches modules on stand-up comedy.

TIERNAN DOUIEB is a comedian, writer, actor, tea drinker, obsessive Tweeter and professional beard wearer. As well as doing friendly, political stand-up for adults all over the world, he co-runs the Comedy Club 4 Kids and regularly shouts jokes at children. Tiernan has watched *Spaced* at least 452 times. Probably.

JANE DUFFUS is a journalist and author who set up the What The Frock! Comedy brand in January 2012 after growing fed up by the lack of women in most comedy clubs or on TV and radio shows. As well as being a monthly night in Bristol, there are also What The Frock! Comedy shows in Bath, London, Manchester and Exeter, as well as various solo shows, improv theatre and an all-female comedy competition.

PAUL DUFFUS received his PhD in literature and critical theory from the University of Bristol. He performed stand-up comedy in the late 1990s to narrow acclaim. He currently writes for various websites and is working on his first novel.

VIV GROSKOP is a writer, performer and author of acclaimed comedy memoir *I Laughed, I Cried*. She began her career on *Cosmopolitan* and worked as a columnist and arts writer at the *Guardian* and the *London Evening Standard* before taking up stand-up comedy in her late thirties.

JOANNE HOLLOWS is a writer and researcher who works on food, feminism and domestic culture (not necessarily at the same time). Her books include *Feminism, Femininity and Popular Culture*, *Domestic Cultures* and *Food and Cultural Studies*.

ANDREW HUNTER MURRAY is a writer and comedian. He spends his days working as a researcher on *QI* and as a journalist at *Private Eye* magazine, and his evenings performing both solo and in *Austentatious*: an improvised Jane Austen comedy show.

ANDREW KELLY is Director of Bristol Cultural Development Partnership and Bristol Festival of Ideas. He is the author/editor of 12 books, four on the history of cinema. He has programmed film seasons at the National Film Theatre, Watershed and Arnolfini.

JESS MCCABE is a journalist and former editor of *The F-Word*, an online feminist magazine. These days she writes about social housing and the welfare state, sustainability and progressive feminism. Her work has been published in lots of places, including *The Guardian*, *Bitch Magazine* and *Women's eNews*.

IAN MARTIN is an award-winning writer and consulting producer for the Emmy-winning HBO series *Veep*, and a writer for the BAFTA-winning BBC series *The Thick Of It*. He was also a writer on the Oscar-nominated 2009 film *In The Loop*. Ian is the author of *The Coalition Chronicles*.

JAMES MULLINGER is Comedy Editor at *GQ* magazine and the only male stand-up with a degree in Women's Studies. A proud feminist he has toured the UK with his show *The Bad Boy Of Feminism,* which culminated with a sold out West End run at the Soho Theatre.

RHODRI MARSDEN is a writer, author and musician. He has been a columnist for *The Independent* since 2005, and has written about technology, social media, music, food, anxiety, relationships and various ephemera for many publications including *The Guardian*, *The Observer*, *Shortlist*, *Time Out* and many others. He plays in Scritti Politti and a TV theme tribute band called Dream Themes.

AMY MASON writes books and makes funny, sometimes painfully honest, autobiographical performances. Her novel *The Other Ida* won the 2014 Dundee International Book Prize. Her new show *Mass*, about her relationship with faith, is in development with Bristol Old Vic, and her previous show, lo-fi musical *The Islanders,* was winner of the 2013 Ideas Tap/Underbelly Edinburgh Fringe Fund.

CERYS NELMES is a comedian from the West Country. She lives at home with her teenage son and their multiple chihuahuas. She has lived a colourful life and worked in various occupations including firefighter, chef and florist, before finding her true vocation in comedy. Cerys is a resident compere with What The Frock! Comedy.

MARINA O'SHEA is a comedian, mother, writer, actor and dancer. Marina tours the UK as the funny one in O'Shea & O'Gaukroger. She was discovered at the age of nine and has been encouraged to continue being an idiot since then. She's dead serious. But people just keep laughing.

BOBBIE OLIVER is a comedian, writer and comedy teacher from Athens, Georgia, currently living and working in Los Angeles. Bobbie is the owner of Tao Comedy Studio in LA and the author of *The Tao of Comedy: Embrace the Pause.*

NAOMI PAXTON is an actor, researcher and character comedian and has appeared in the West End and on tour in the UK and internationally. She performs as Ada Campe, completed her PhD at the University of Manchester and edited *The Methuen Drama Book of Suffrage Plays*. Naomi was one of the AHRC/BBC Radio 3's 'New Generation Thinkers' for 2014.

LUCY PORTER is a comedian and writer with three sold-out stand-up tours to her name so far. She is a regular on TV and radio panel shows, including *Have I Got News For You*, *Never Mind The Buzzcocks* and *Mock The Week*. She was the winner of a special edition of *Celebrity Mastermind* – breaking records by achieving the highest ever celebrity score. Her specialist subject? Steve Martin.

CHELLA QUINT is a comedy writer and performer originally from Brooklyn, New York, who now lives in Sheffield, England (she swears they are very similar). She regularly performs science communication comedy, hosts *Comedy in Space*, edits *Adventures in Menstruating*, and is a big fan of dinosaurs, wind turbines and intersectional feminism.

TIMON SINGH is an editor and a full time film geek who runs The Bristol Bad Film Club. If he could be bothered, he'd write a script where Jennifer Lawrence, Kristin Bell and Emma Stone are a trio of sassy space-age bounty hunters... but he's really lazy.

KATE SMURTHWAITE is a slick, intelligent, political and observational comedian. She is also a regular writer for TV shows including *Have I Got News For You* and *The Revolution Will Be Televised*. Her annual *News At Kate* and *Comedy Manifesto* Edinburgh shows attract a devoted following. Kate has worked closely with What The Frock! Comedy since it launched.

GABRIELA STANISZEWSKA is a filmmaker, cat owner and chicken herder. Resolutely uptight and misanthropic, she likes watching movies, cooking and gardening. She has produced several short films, and is currently working on a documentary about women in comedy. Gabriela has been directly involved with What The Frock! Comedy from day one.

ESTELLA TINCKNELL is Associate Professor in Film and Culture at the University of the West of England. She has published widely in the areas of film, media and popular culture and has a particular interest in representations of older women on screen as a member of the Women, Aging, Media network. She contributes a film column to the TUC blog *Aging Matters*, and edits the film and music journal *The Soundtrack*.

DANIELLE WARD is a writer, comedian and actor. She first shot to fame aged four when she had her photo taken for the local paper with a man who was doing some cycling thing. Maybe he was taking part in the Tour De France. She has forgotten the details. Since then she's written two musicals, a BBC Radio 4 series, a sitcom and a declining number of postcards to her grandmother.

ROSIE WILBY has performed in New York, Sydney and all over the UK with solo shows *The Science Of Sex*, *Nineties Woman*, *Is Monogamy Dead?* and *How (Not) To Make It In Britpop*. She appears on various BBC Radio 4 shows and at festivals including Glastonbury, Latitude and Larmer Tree and in print in *The Sunday Times*, *The Independent*, *Diva* and Accent Press anthology *It's OK To Be Gay*.

LOUISE WINGROVE is a PhD student as the University of Bristol examining the success of female comedians in the Victorian Music Hall and the use of humour in the fight for women's suffrage. Having performed herself, Louise is also interested in the ongoing development of stand-up comedy and women's success within the industry.

BIBLIOGRAPHY

This is a far-from-comprehensive list of books, but these are some suggestions of (auto)biographies about women in comedy, books about women and the comedy industry more generally, and other books spelling out the gross gender inequalities women are facing more widely. Which tie back into many of the issues facing women working in comedy. And there are two novels in there as well, because women being funny has even been the subject of a few fictitious tales (both of those listed here are based on real life funny women, mind you).

Feel free to contact What The Frock! Comedy and let us know of any blindingly glaring omissions, and we'll be happy to update this list in any future editions of this book. You can email: jane@whatthefrockcomedy.co.uk

BATES, LAURA – *Everyday Sexism* (Simon & Schuster, 2014)

BRAND, KATY – *Brenda Monk Is Funny* (Unbound, 2014)

DENT, GRACE – *How To Leave Twitter: My Time As Queen of The Universe And Why This Must Stop* (Faber & Faber, 2011)

DOUBLE, OLIVER – *Getting The Joke: The Inner Workings of Stand-Up Comedy* (Bloomsbury, 2013)

DUNHAM, LENA – *Not That Kind Of Girl* (Fourth Estate, 2014)

FEY, TINA – *Bossypants* (Sphere, 2011)

FREEMAN, HADLEY – *Be Awesome* (Fourth Estate, 2013)

GROSKOP, VIV – *I Laughed, I Cried: How One Woman Took On Stand-Up And (Almost) Ruined Her Life* (Orion, 2013)

HORNBY, NICK – *Funny Girl* (Penguin, 2014)

HOROWITZ, SUSAN – *Queens Of Comedy* (Routledge, 1997)

KALING, MINDY – *Is Everybody Hanging Out Without Me?* (Ebury Press, 2011)

KOHEN, YAEL – *We Killed: The Rise of Women in American Comedy* (Picador, 2013)

MIZEJEWSKI, LINDA – *Pretty/Funny: Women Comedians and Body Politics* (Texas University Press, 2014)

OLIVER, BOBBIE – *The Tao Of Comedy: Embrace The Pause* (CreateSpace, 2013)

POEHLER, AMY – *Yes Please* (Picador, 2014)

WALKER, NANCY A – *A Very Serious Thing: Women's Humor and American Culture* (University of Minnesota Press, 1988)

WAX, RUBY – *How Do You Want Me?* (Ebury Press, 2002)

SAUNDERS, JENNIFER – *Bonkers* (Penguin, 2013)

SMITH, LINDA – *I Think The Nurses Are Stealing My Clothes…* (Hodder, 2006)

WHITE, BETTY – *Here We Go Again: My Life In Television* (Scribner, 1995)

The following websites are also useful resources:

Chortle – www.chortle.co.uk

Funny Women – www.funnywomen.com

Laughing Cows – www.laughingcowscomedy.co.uk

What The Frock! Comedy – www.whatthefrockcomedy.co.uk

ACKNOWLEDGEMENTS

I say 'we' when I talk about What The Frock! but it's a royal 'we' because it sounds somewhat arrogant to keep saying 'I' and 'me'. However, it's impossible to do anything like this without help. So I must thank: **Jayde Adams, Cerys Nelmes, Viv Groskop, Naomi Paxton, Lucy Porter** and **Kate Smurthwaite** for being outrageously funny women and for becoming friends who've gone beyond the pale in supporting What The Frock! Comedy. Some other supersonic individuals are: **Emily Coles** (photographer), **Jenny Éclair** (comedian), **Martin Evans** (BBC Bristol), **Andrew Kelly** (Bristol Festival of Ideas), **Caroline Mornement** (publisher), **Laura Rawlings** (BBC Bristol)… oh, I could be here all day.

And, of course, I must thank each and every one of the 28 people who contributed their thoughts about their own favourite comedian to this book. All of whom are busy people with their own projects and work, so I am genuinely touched and grateful that they took the time to indulge mine. Thank you so much.

More than anyone, I unreservedly thank three people:

Paul Duffus – who married me before I dreamt up the idea for What The Frock!, and as such is within his rights to be fed up at the inordinate amount of time his wife spends on her laptop or out at comedy clubs. But instead he champions What The Frock!, comes up with brilliant ideas to grow the brand, and cooks the dinner when I'm working late.

Gabriela Staniszewska – who never says 'no' to me, even when she should, and who has championed What The Frock! with more enthusiasm than I ever thought possible from another human being.

Emily Turner – who creates our logos, artwork, flyers and this very book you're reading right now. Emily is a design wizard and as such is quite rightly the Creative Director of What The Frock!